COPING WITH SELF ASSESSMENT

How To Books on business and management

Be a Freelance Sales Agent
Buy & Run a Shop
Buy & Run a Small Hotel
Communicate at Work
Conduct Staff Appraisals
Conducting Effective Interviews
Coping with Self Assessment
Doing Business Abroad
Do Your Own Advertising
Do Your Own PR
Employ & Manage Staff
Investing in Stocks & Shares
Keep Business Accounts
Manage a Sales Team
Manage an Office
Manage Computers at Work
Manage People at Work
Managing Budgets & Cash Flows
Managing Meetings
Managing Yourself

Market Yourself
Master Book-Keeping
Master Public Speaking
Organising Effective Training
Prepare a Business Plan
Publish a Book
Publish a Newsletter
Raise Business Finance
Sell Your Business
Start a Business from Home
Start Your Own Business
Starting to Manage
Successful Mail Order Marketing
Taking on Staff
Understand Finance at Work
Use the Internet
Winning Presentations
Write a Report
Write Business Letters
Write & Sell Computer Software

Further titles in preparation

The How To series now contains more than 200 titles in the following categories:

Business Basics
Family Reference
Jobs & Careers
Living & Working Abroad
Student Handbooks
Successful Writing

Please send for a free copy of the latest catalogue for full details
(see back cover for address).

BUSINESS BASICS

COPING WITH
SELF ASSESSMENT

How to complete your tax return
and pay less tax

John Whiteley

How To Books

Acknowledgements

Crown Copyright material is reproduced with the permission of the Controller of HMSO.

The illustrations of the cartoon character in this book are reproduced by permission of the Inland Revenue. The author has made every effort to check the accuracy of the text. Use of the Self Assessment logo and the cartoon character does not imply endorsement by the Inland Revenue of the accuracy of the content.

Disclaimer

Neither the author nor the publishers can be held responsible for any action taken or refrained from being taken as a result of the contents of this book.

British Library Cataloguing in Publication Data

A catalogue record for this book is available from the British Library.

© Copyright 1997 by John Whiteley.

First published in 1997 by How To Books Ltd, 3 Newtec Place, Magdalen Road, Oxford OX4 1RE, United Kingdom.
Tel: (01865) 793806. Fax: (01865) 248780.

Note: The material contained in this book is set out in good faith for general guidance and no liability can be accepted for loss or expense incurred as a result of relying in particular circumstances on statements made in the book. The laws and regulations are complex and liable to change, and readers should check the current position with the relevant authorities before making personal arrangements.

Produced for How To Books by Deer Park Productions.
Typeset by PDQ Typesetting, Stoke-on-Trent, Staffs.
Printed and bound by Cromwell Press, Broughton Gifford, Melksham, Wiltshire.

Contents

List of Illustrations

Preface

Self assessment is not a new tax, but it is, in the words of the Inland Revenue; 'a clearer and more efficient way of calculating and paying tax'. Self assessment already existed in one form or another in many countries before it was introduced in the UK.

An estimated 8.5 million self assessment tax returns will have been sent out for the first time in April 1997. Although the Inland Revenue describes this as 'a clearer and more efficient way of calculating and paying tax', many people will be dismayed at the sheer volume and complexity of the new tax returns. There are also strict rules about the records which must be kept, and a new regime of automatic penalties, interest and surcharges.

This book helps you to understand the tax system, and takes you step by step through the process of filling in the tax return and paying the tax. Other chapters deal with the record keeping requirements, and how to avoid penalties, interest and surcharges.

We all want to save tax, and a final chapter deals with some key strategies for minimising your tax bill without breaking the law.

As a Chartered Accountant, and a partner in a practice, I deal with tax affairs for a wide variety of clients. I have drawn on many years' experience to bring you practical help in coping with self assessment.

John Whiteley

1
Adapting to the Change

UNDERSTANDING THE OLD SYSTEM

Before the self assessment system came along, there were three steps to the tax system:

- filling in a tax return
- receiving a tax assessment
- paying the tax.

Filling in the tax return

The tax return was usually issued on 6 April each year. Strictly, the tax return should have been returned within 30 days, but in practice the Inland Revenue treated returns submitted by 31 October as 'on time'. Some taxpayers had repayments of tax year after year and their affairs were dealt with by specialist repayment districts. These districts will continue to deal with the repayment cases.

Receiving the assessment

When the Inspector of Taxes received the return, he would make an assessment. Sometimes the assessment was estimated.

Schedule A assessments were for property income. Schedule D

assessments were for either self employed income or untaxed interest. A schedule E assessment was for income from employment. This income had tax deducted under PAYE, but occasionally there would be adjustments, due to such things as incorrect estimates of certain items or an expenses claim.

A higher rate assessment was made for income which had already been taxed at source (such as dividends or bank interest) and which was liable to the higher rate of tax.

A capital gains assessment was issued for capital gains.

Making an appeal

On receipt of an assessment, the taxpayer had to check that it was correct. If not, then you could make an appeal against it, stating the reason for the appeal, and you could also apply for a postponement of all or part of the tax assessed.

Paying the tax

The assessment would state exactly when the tax was due to be paid, and the payment slip attached to the form could be used as a bank giro credit.

If tax was paid late, interest could be charged, but this was not always applied.

In the case of a schedule E assessment, any overpayment would have been repaid to you, and any underpayment would have been adjusted on the following year's code number, so that it was collected over the next year.

COPING WITH THE NEW SYSTEM

The new system retains some features of the old system. The main difference is that the Inspector of Taxes will no longer issue assessments.

The tax return itself is also the basis for your own self assessment of your tax liability, and your means of calculating the payments of tax that are due.

The tax return

The tax return will continue to be issued on 6 April, but now there are two dates for sending it in. If you want to make your own calculation of tax, you have until the following **31 January** to send it in. If you want the Inspector of Taxes to calculate the tax, send it in by **30 September**.

By filling in all the boxes in the tax return and the calculation working sheet, you arrive at a figure of tax you owe, taking into account what has already been deducted from you, what you have already paid on account, and what is due to be paid on account for the next year.

Thus, all the features of the old system are within the one-step operation of the new system.

CASE STUDIES

Introduction

Anthony
Anthony (46) is self employed, running a shoe shop in the centre of a small town. He and his wife (42) live in a flat above the shop. He employs his wife in the business, and one other part time assistant. He is paying premiums to a pension policy. His business is his main source of income, but he has a building society account, and some shares in two of the privatisation issues – his local electricity company, and British Telecom. His wife also has a building society account in her own name.

Max
Max (76) is retired. He receives a company pension from his former employer, as well as the state pension. He has accounts with three different building societies, and a bank premium account which gives him interest. He has a portfolio of shares worth about £50,000, and also a portfolio of five different unit trusts worth about £20,000.

His wife (70) also receives a state pension, but no other pension. She also has a couple of building society accounts, National Savings Income Bonds worth £5,000, and a unit trust investment worth about £5,000.

Yvonne
Yvonne (35) is single, and a director of a company which runs an advertising agency. Her salary is in the region of £25,000 per year, and she has a company car, and other benefits such as private medical insurance. She also owns 100 shares in the company. She owns her own house, on which she has a mortgage. She also owns a house which she inherited, and which she lets out on a long term letting.

Anthony uses an accountant

Anthony has an accountant who completed his tax returns under the old system. The accountant also checked the assessment issued by the Inspector of Taxes, and made appeals as necessary. He also advised Anthony of the correct amounts to pay, and the due dates.

Under the new system, Anthony will continue to get his accountant to deal with his tax affairs, helping with filling in the tax return, checking payment dates *etc.*

Max opts for self reliance

Max filled in his own tax return under the old system. He checked the assessments as far as he could, but he was sometimes baffled by them. Unless there was any glaring error, he paid the amounts demanded.

Under the new system, he will fill in his own tax return and calculate his own tax. He is slightly mistrustful, and is uneasy about asking the Inspector of Taxes to work out his tax. He feels confident about his ability to get things right. He is an organised sort of person, and keeps his filing up to date.

Yvonne get help

Yvonne has always filled in her own tax return until now. She has always paid the tax due on her property income assessment issued by the Inspector of Taxes, believing it to be right.

She is now considering getting the company accountant to help with her tax affairs, since she is a little overawed by self assessment.

DISCUSSION POINTS

1. Will the new system mean that you change the way you deal with your tax returns?

2. Is your filing system and general organisation adequate to keep you sufficiently up to date?

3. Will you ask the Inspector of Taxes to carry out the calculations? If so, are you able to fill in your part of the tax return by 30 September?

2
Keeping Records
for the Self Employed

SETTING UP AN ADEQUATE SYSTEM

Until the new self assessment system, there was no legal requirement for income tax purposes to keep records of business dealings. It is, of course, common sense to keep records, so that you know how your business is performing. You may also keep records for VAT purposes.

What records are required by law?
The law requires you to keep such records as are needed to make a complete and correct return. For a **business**, this specifically includes:

- all amounts received and spent in the business, and a description of the receipts and expenses

- all sales and purchases of goods in the trade (where the business involves trading in goods).

What records will be adequate in practice?
The legal requirements are obviously not a complete guide to what you need to keep to provide an adequate record of your business.

Each business has its own requirements, but all businesses should have:

(a) book-keeping records
(b) a filing system for records.

Although it is not a legal requirement, a business benefits greatly from having its own bank account. If you are in business on your own, open a separate business bank account, and keep all private transactions in your private bank account.

Book-keeping
The book-keeping system should enable you to identify:

- all sales and other income of the business
- purchases of goods for sale and other business expenses
- purchases and sales of assets used in your business
- all amounts taken from the business, whether by cash, cheque or goods in kind
- all amounts put in the business from your personal sources
- private proportions of business expenses such as motor expenses
- values of stock and work in progress at the year end.

Filing
The filing system should enable you to access easily the important documents backing up the book-keeping system. This would include such items as:

- bank statements
- building society statements
- sales invoices
- purchases invoices
- expenses invoices
- petty cash vouchers
- wages and PAYE records
- mileage records
- stock-taking sheets.

Book-keeping in detail
The exact type of book-keeping system will depend on the type of business you are in. A basic minimum would be:

1. Cash book.
2. Petty cash book.

If you are running a business with no credit sales, and no employees, such as a small retail shop, these could be all the books you need. The cash book and the petty cash book could be the types with analysis columns (you can buy these in any good commercial stationer). Use the analysis columns to analyse the different types of receipts and expenditure.

Analysis of receipts
Usually, there are fewer types of receipts to analyse than expenses.

For many small retail businesses, two columns are adequate – one for sales, the other for any other type of receipt. Other businesses may have receipts of different sorts to analyse, and the degree of analysis depends on how complex your business is. You may want to break down your sales between different types of goods. This may even be necessary for VAT purposes. A typical village general store, for example, may break down its sales between:

- food
- drinks
- stationery
- sweets
- Lottery tickets
- tobacco
- other goods.

There may be other ways of analysing sales – for example among different geographical areas, including exports; between different salesmen; mail order businesses may want to analyse the response between different advertising sources. The way in which you analyse the receipts depends on:

- your type of business, and
- the information you want.

Your book-keeping system is mainly for your own needs, but the more information you have, the better you will be able to satisfy the requirements of the Inland Revenue. Figure 1 gives an example of a simple cash book receipts analysis.

Analysis of payments
Normally there is more analysis for payments than for receipts. Break down the payments into the expenses of the business, purchase of assets for the business, and money you take out of the business.

RECEIPTS ANALYSIS

	DATE	DESCRIPTION	1 AMOUNT	2 TYPE 1 SALES	3 TYPE 2 SALES	4 LOTTERY TICKETS	5 OTHER RECEIPTS	6
1	1.3.97	TAKINGS	165 10	100 50	38 60	26 00		
2	2.3.97	TAKINGS	113 50	98 20	15 30			
3	3.3.97	FROM PRIVATE BANK	200 00				200 00	
4	4.3.97	TAKINGS	149 90	110 30	29 60	10 00		
5	4.3.97	INSURANCE CLAIM	550 00				550 00	
6	5.3.97	TAKINGS	181 60	126 40	40 20	15 00		
7								
8		TOTALS	1360 10	435 40	123 10	51 00	750 00	
9								

Fig. 1. Sample receipts analysis.

	DATE	DESCRIPTION	1 AMOUNT	2 RESALE GOODS	3 OVERHEADS	4 ASSETS	5 PRIVATE	6
1	1.3.97	A.B.C. LTD	120 00	120 00				
2	3.3.97	RATES	50 50		50 50			
3	3.3.97	CAR PURCHASED	1,500 00			1500 00		
4	4.3.97	OWN DRAWINGS	100 00				100 00	
5	5.3.97	X.Y.Z. LTD	150 60	150 60				
6	5.3.97	CAR INSURANCE	200 00		200 00			
7								
8		TOTALS	2,121 10	270 60	250 50	1500 00	100 00	
9								

Fig. 2. Sample payments analysis.

Expenses of the business need to be broken down into the categories on page SE2 of the tax return (see Figure 4), even if you need a different analysis for your own purposes. Figure 2 shows a simple analysis of payments.

Other book-keeping records

If your business has credit sales, you should keep a **sales day book**, detailing all sales, showing the invoice number, the name of the customer, and the amount of the goods, VAT and the total. You also need a sales ledger, showing the amount owing to you from each customer at any time.

Most businesses buy goods from their suppliers on credit, and you may find it useful to keep a **purchase day book** and purchase ledger. This works in the same way as a sales day book and sales ledger, and shows how much you owe to each supplier.

If you employ anybody in your business, you need a **wages book**, showing the gross amount of each person's wages, the deductions for tax, national insurance, any other deductions, the net amount paid, and the employer's contribution to National Insurance. You also need to keep the Inland Revenue PAYE records to enable you to pay over the right amounts for PAYE and National Insurance.

WRITING UP THE BOOKS

It is all very well having a good system of book-keeping, but if the records are not accurate, then even the best system in the world is not worth much.

Don't put it off!

One of the best ways to ensure that your records are as accurate as they can be is to write them up **regularly and frequently**. If your business is not big enough to employ a book-keeper or an accountant, then writing up the books is one of the chores that often gets left until a later time. That 'later time' can get put back even further if an unexpected crisis occurs, or if you just feel too tired. You are then faced with a mammoth task which in itself is daunting. This can lead to rushing the job, or not giving it the attention it needs. That is when mistakes most easily occur.

Put aside a time regularly to write up your books. If you can't manage a time every day, find the time once or twice a week. Make it a regular spot in your diary, and you will get into a routine. You will find that doing the job regularly and frequently means that it is cut down into manageable chunks.

Try, if possible, to be away from the phone – if there is someone who can look after the business during your 'book-keeping' time, that minimises distractions. Of course, with a one man business, the book-keeping and other administrative duties are often done at home in the evenings.

KEEPING A COMPUTERISED SYSTEM

As more people become computer literate, computerised book-keeping systems are becoming more popular. Book-keeping systems and personal financial programs are amongst the best selling computer software products.

With such a wide choice, there should be no problem in finding the program to suit your needs. However, just as a desk top publisher does not transform you into a graphic designer, an accounting program will not turn you into an accountant. If you already have an accountant, do talk to him about it before you actually buy a program. If you want to 'go it alone', then ask yourself the following questions about any system you are looking at:

1. Does it produce a balanced set of figures automatically?
2. Does it work on double entry book-keeping principles?
3. Does it produce a detailed audit trail?
4. Does it allow you to tailor the analysis of receipts and payments?
5. Does it show you what you owe to suppliers and what you are owed by customers?

If the system does all these things, it goes a long way to providing what you need. Even with a computerised system, you still need the self discipline to write up the system regularly and frequently.

COVERING ALL THE ANGLES

Whether you have a manual or a computerised system, there are many angles which you need to make sure you cover systematically. These are items which will not necessarily be the subject of a cash or cheque transaction. Here are some of the things you need to think about and account for:

Taking goods for your own and family use
If you pay for these at their full value, no further records are needed. Otherwise, you should make sure that you account for these items properly. They should be added to your sales both for income tax purposes and for VAT purposes.

Supplying goods for business purposes
These should also be added to sales, and can also be deducted as a
business expense. An example of this would be a publican who
supplies drinks or refreshments to a darts or skittles team.

Exchanging
This means goods or services supplied to someone in exchange for
goods or services from them when no money changes hands. Once
again, these items should form part of your sales. The goods or
services for which you exchanged them, however, may form part of
the expenses of the business.

Private use
Some assets are used partly for business use and partly for private
use. You should keep adequate records to enable you to justify to
the Inspector of Taxes the part you are claiming as a business
expense. The most obvious example of this is your car. Keep a note
book in the car to record mileage of business trips and private trips.
These are totalled for the year and the running costs can be split
between business and private use. Another example is telephone
expenses. If you get an itemised bill, it is not difficult to separate
business from private use.

Private accommodation
If you live on the same premises as the business, the expenses of the
property should be split between private and business use. For most
items, this does not pose a great problem. It is usually easy to get gas,
electricity and water metered separately. Council tax is billed for
domestic premises and business rates are levied on business property.

Paying expenses for the business
You may often find that you pay for business expenses out of your
own pocket, or even out of your own private bank or building
society account. Make sure you bring these into account as a
business expense.

Taking stock
Keep records of your stock-take. This is usually carried out
annually, but you may take stock more frequently. Stock should
always be valued for your accounts at the lower of its cost or its
present market value.

Adjustments

Adjust for creditors, accruals and prepayments. This is because accounts for tax purposes have to be prepared on what is known as the **accruals basis**. This means that all income and expenditure has to be matched to the right accounts year. This may seem obvious, but some payments are not made in the year to which they relate. For example, insurance is normally paid for a year in advance. So, if you paid insurance on 1 March, and your year end is 31 March, only one month of that payment relates to the current year, and eleven months relate to the next year.

Similarly, some expenses such as electricity bills are paid quarterly, but in arrears. Therefore, if your year end is on 31 March, and your electricity meter was read on that day, the bill will not be sent until some time in April, and the payment for electricity for the last three months of the year will not be paid until the following year.

Adjustments need to be made at the beginning and the end of the year for these items, known as prepayments (or payments in advance) and creditors (or accruals).

RETAINING YOUR RECORDS

You must keep the accounting records for **five years** from the latest date for filing your tax return which includes your business accounts.

Example

Your business year end is 31 May. The accounts for the year ended 31 May 1997 will be included in the tax return for the year ended 5 April 1998. The latest date for filing that tax return is 31 January 1999. You must therefore keep the records safe until 31 January 2004.

If the Inspector of Taxes is making an enquiry into your tax return, you must keep the records until you have been notified that the enquiry has been completed. In exceptional circumstances, this could mean your keeping records longer than the five year limit mentioned above.

You need therefore to have enough space to keep all the records and a way of identifying them for each year. Usually a box with a label on is quite adequate, unless your business records are more bulky.

Penalties

If you do not produce adequate records, or if you do not keep them for the required period, the Inland Revenue can charge you with a **penalty**. In the most extreme cases, the penalty charged could be

£3,000 for each failure to write up or retain adequate records to back up a tax return.

If you are charged with a penalty, you have the right to **appeal** against the penalty.

QUESTIONS AND ANSWERS

My bank charges a lot more for business bank accounts than for private accounts. Is it really necessary to have a separate business and private bank account?

Unless your business is really small, you probably benefit by having a separate business bank account. You could also try negotiating the price for bank charges with your bank manager.

Many building societies have cheque accounts which make little or no charges, or you could also open a giro account. This could be an advantage where the amounts of cash and notes are significant. If all else fails, you can use a single account for your business and your private transactions. But this means that you have to record all your private receipts and payments in your book-keeping records. If you use an accountant, this could mean that it gives him more work, and his fees are more.

Virtually all my suppliers invoice me and I pay on monthly accounts with them. Do I really have to keep a purchases day book and a purchases ledger?

If you have a system that will enable you to keep track of what you owe to your suppliers then a day book and a ledger are not strictly necessary. You may, for instance, keep all your suppliers' invoices in alphabetical order in a 'concertina type' file, until they are paid. Then when you pay them, write the date of payment on each one, and write the cheque in the cash book. At the same time, transfer the paid invoices to a file for paid invoices, which could be in date order or in alphabetical order.

I often have to pay cash items out of the till before I can bank the money from takings. How do I account for this?

Keep a pad of petty cash vouchers by the till (you can get these at most stationers). Then, when you make a payment from the till, write out a voucher and put it in the till. At the end of the day, when you are cashing up, count these as if they were cash. You will then have a total for takings, from which you deduct the expenses paid to arrive at the amount left available for banking.

CASE STUDY

Anthony keeps adequate accounts

Anthony runs a shoe shop, with no sales on credit. He likes to keep a record of sales of accessories, such as handbags, socks, tights, polishes and brushes *etc.* His till is able to give readings of sales under the two categories – shoes and accessories.

He pays by cheque for the main suppliers and the main items of overheads. He keeps a petty cash tin, and pays small incidentals from that. He has a business bank account and a private bank account. He transfers from his business bank account to his private bank account regularly, and pays his normal living expenses from his private bank account. However, he pays his income tax and his pension premiums from the business account.

Anthony's business records consist of:

- main cash book, showing the receipts and payments from the business bank account
- petty cash book
- stock-taking records
- a record of goods taken from the shop for private and family use
- mileage records for the car
- wages book for his part time employee and his wife.

The cash book shows his analysis of the different categories of receipts, including the shop sales (divided between shoes and accessories) and any private money put into the business.

The payments side of the cash book shows the payments broken down between purchases of goods for resale, expenses of the business, purchase of assets for the business (such as equipment, car *etc*) and private monies taken out of the business. The expenses of the business are separated into the different categories on the tax return. He bought a cash book with more columns to enable this degree of analysis.

He keeps the following documents, properly filed:

- business account bank statements
- cheque book stubs
- paying-in book stubs
- invoices for cheque payments made

- till rolls for the receipts
- petty cash vouchers.

Once the accounts have been prepared and entered on the tax return, he bundles up all the documents, puts them in a large box, labels it with the year, and puts it in his loft for storage.

DISCUSSION POINTS

1. How would you go about deciding what degree of sophistication you need in a book-keeping system?

2. Think about your work pattern. Is there a specific time each day, each week, each month which you could set aside for book-keeping and administrative work? When would you reach the 'critical point' at which it would pay you to employ a book-keeper, while you go out and earn money?

3. Think about the information you would like to help you run your business better and make the right decisions. What is the critical factor in your business – sales volume, sales mix, controlling the costs, getting the right grade of employees, or something else? How could you tailor your book-keeping system to provide you with the right information?

CREATING YOUR OWN RECORDS

Some records of transactions will come from some other source, and all you need to do is keep them safely. However, you need to create some records yourself.

As a general rule, make a record of some sort for any type of income which is *not* supported by a document sent to you with the income. This could include:

For employed people:
    records of tips, gratuities, *etc.*

For share schemes:
    notes of share prices on the relevant dates.

Property income:
    record of rents received
    record of expenses.

Capital gains:
    record of sales of assets
    valuations carried out of assets
    share prices quoted on the stock exchange.

KEEPING RECORDS ORIGINATING FROM ELSEWHERE

Many types of income will be accompanied by a document of some
sort when you receive it. You must keep these documents. They
would include the following:

For an employed person
- P60 – the year end statement showing your earnings and the tax
  deducted
- P45 – if you left a job during the tax year
- P160 – if you retired from an employment and your former
  employer paid you a pension
- payslips
- forms P11D or P9D – forms showing benefits from your
  employment and expenses paid to you
- receipts for expenses you are claiming
- PAYE coding notices.

For share options
- correspondence from the company
- exercise note
- information on the share prices on relevant dates.

For property income
- agent's statements of rents collected
- rent books
- receipts for expenses.

For overseas income
- statements of amounts you received
- foreign tax receipts or certificates.

For trust income
- R185 certificates from the trustees.

For capital gains
- contracts for the sale of the assets
- brokers' notes for sales of shares
- copies of any valuations carried out on the assets
- details of the original acquisition of the assets sold
- published figures for indexation allowance.

For savings and investment income
- bank statements
- certificates of interest from banks or building societies
- statements of National Savings interest
- dividend vouchers from shares and unit trusts
- interest vouchers from government stocks or loan stocks.

For pensions and Social Security benefits
- P60 showing the occupational pension and tax deducted
- details of Social Security pensions and benefits – the first page of order books give these details
- PAYE coding notices.

For other income
- correspondence relating to maintenance or alimony
- certificates from life assurance companies of chargeable gains
- any correspondence relating to other income.

For residence and domicile
- any correspondence, travel tickets, passports *etc* which show your movements
- any evidence showing where your permanent home is.

For allowances and reliefs
- certificates of pension premiums paid
- charitable deeds of covenant
- certificates for venture capital trusts
- certificates for Enterprise Investment Scheme relief
- birth certificate where age is a factor
- marriage certificate where you are claiming married couple's allowance for the first time
- death certificate where you are claiming widow's bereavement allowance
- evidence of your child's education if you are claiming additional personal allowance and the child is over 16
- registration as a blind person
- certificates of interest paid.

FILING YOUR RECORDS

It would obviously not be very helpful to simply throw all the documents into a carrier bag, or even into a drawer in a desk. Buy yourself a few folders or files, and arrange your records according to the type of income. Then, when the time comes to fill in your tax return, you will have everything to hand to deal with each section. Within each section, it is also useful to keep to some sort of order where there are large numbers of documents. For example, if you have many investments in shares or unit trusts, file them in alphabetical order, so that you can find any one easily.

RETAINING YOUR RECORDS

In normal circumstances, you need to retain your records for **22 months** after the end of the tax year to which they relate. This applies when you send the tax return in within the normal time limit.

If you send your tax return in late you will have to keep the records for two years after the date you sent your tax return in.

If the Inland Revenue sent you your tax return later than the normal date, you have three months to fill it in and send it back (if that is later than the normal filing date). In that case, you must retain your records for a year from that filing date.

If you are undergoing an Inland Revenue investigation, you must keep all the records until the Inland Revenue tells you that you need no longer retain them.

Examples

1. You received your tax return on 6 April 1997. You sent it back on 31 October 1997. The normal filing date is 31 January 1998, and you must retain your records until 31 January 1999.

2. You received your tax return on 6 April 1997. You sent it back on 28 February 1998. You were late, and you must retain your records until 28 February 2000.

3. You received your tax return on 1 January 1998. You sent it back on 28 February 1998, *ie* before the filing date of 31 March 1998. You must retain your records until 31 March 1999.

Warning
If you receive property income, that is treated in the same way as self employed income. You must retain your records for **five years** from the normal filing date.

QUESTIONS AND ANSWERS

I have not received a P60 from my employer, nor a copy of the P11D benefits. What should I do?

Your employer has an obligation to send you the P60 by 31 May following the year end, and the P11D by 6 July following the year end. You should insist on receiving these, if you do not get them by these dates. If the employer is still not able to give them, the tax office can bring pressure to bear.

I have sold some shares. I have the details of the sale prices and the purchase prices. Where can I get hold of the indexation figures?

The indexation figures are printed in the notes to the capital gains pages. If you need a figure which is not shown there, ask your tax office.

CASE STUDIES

Max keeps adequate records

Max is very organised, and has a filing cabinet at home. He keeps his tax papers filed, with separate folders for his company pension, keeping the coding notice, all his monthly payslips, and his P60. His state pension is paid every four weeks through his bank account, and he keeps all his bank statements. He keeps a folder for all the interest statements from the bank and the building societies. In another folder he keeps all the dividend vouchers for his shares and his unit trusts.

He likewise keeps a separate folder for all his wife's papers. In this he keeps all her building society interest statements, her National Savings interest statements, and her unit trust dividends.

Yvonne asks for help

Yvonne is not very organised. She has not kept proper records of the rents she receives from the house, nor the expenses against those rents. She has not retained the P60 or the copy of the P11D benefits statement.

When she gets her tax return, she realises that there is quite a bit of work to do to get all the information together, so she gives her bank statements to the company accountant, and asks him to sort out her tax affairs. He is able to get the details of her salary and her P11D benefits from the company records, and he is able to piece together the information relating to her rents. However, she cannot lay her hands on some invoices from builders for repairs to the house, and she has to ask for copies.

DISCUSSION POINTS

1. If you are married, which of you is the better organised? Can you agree on who is to do the administrative work of keeping all the papers in order?

2. Do you need to start making a record in, say, a cash book or a diary, of any financial matters such as share prices, income from property, tips or gratuities received *etc*?

4
Completing the Tax Return Form

RECEIVING THE TAX RETURN FORM

Shortly after 5 April the brown envelope drops through the letter box. From 1997, it will be heavier than previously. In previous years, it consisted of a very short guide, and the tax return form consisted of at most twelve pages. Now there is a guide of thirty pages, a tax form of eight pages, and up to nine supplementary sets of pages, each with their own set of notes.

These supplementary pages deal with the different types of income, such as employment, self employment, partnerships, capital gains, and so on. The good news is that hardly anybody will receive all nine supplementary sets of pages. The Inland Revenue will send the ones they think you need, on the basis of your last return.

Notifying the Inland Revenue if you have not received a tax return

You may not receive a tax return from the Inland Revenue. Should you just be grateful and forget about it? The law says that if you have income which is chargeable to income tax or capital gains tax, and you have not received a tax return, you **must** notify the Inland Revenue of that fact. The time limit for this is six months after the end of the tax year in which you have any such chargeable income or gains – **5 October** is therefore one of the important deadlines.

How do I notify the Inland Revenue?
You should ring or write to your tax office to let them know. But how do you know which is your tax office? Your tax district is the one in whose area your main source of income arises. If you are employed or receive a pension from a former employer, your tax district is the one which deals with the PAYE system. You can easily find out which district this is from your coding notice or your P60 form.

If you are in any doubt, however, contact your local tax office, which will help you find your own tax district.

READING THROUGH THE GUIDE

It may sound obvious to say this, but read through the guide first. You do not have to read through everything, only the sections which apply to your circumstances. Again this may seem obvious, but it is all too easy to start filling things in before reading everything, only to find out later that you have missed something, or entered something wrongly.

Checking that all the right supplementary pages are there
The next job on receiving the tax return form is to check that all the right supplementary pages are there. They consist of:

1. Employment.
2. Share schemes and share option benefits.
3. Self employment for sole traders.
4. Partnership income.
5. Income from land and property in the UK.
6. Foreign income and gains, and tax credit relief.
7. Income from trusts and settlements.
8. Capital gains.
9. Non-residence and non-domicile.

If you have any income under any of these headings, but you do not have the supplementary pages, you must ask your tax office for that section.

Getting help sheets or leaflets
As you read through the guide, you may feel you need more information or help. You may ring or write to them if you feel the query can be easily resolved. If you need more help in under-

standing the subject, the Inland Revenue can send you help sheets or leaflets on that particular topic.

COLLECTING THE INFORMATION

Chapters 2 and 3 dealt in some detail with the records you need to keep. At this stage, you need to arrange all the information so that you can fill in the boxes in the tax return.

Personal details
First of all, make sure that you have all the personal details needed. Apart from your name and address, you may also need:

- your National Insurance number
- if you are claiming Blind Person's Allowance, the name of the local authority under which you are registered as blind.

The Tax Return Form
Figure 3 shows page 2 of the tax return form.

If you answer 'yes' to any of the questions, you are directed to the supplementary pages. If you have income under any of the headings, the following are the items of information you need.

Employment
- the P60 from your employment
- details of any other amounts not on your P60 (such as tips)
- details of benefits and expenses received by you: these are on your P11D
- details of lump sums, compensation or termination payments received
- details of dates you were working abroad
- details of expenses you claim.

If you had more than one employment you will have one P60 for each. You should receive all P60s by 31 May at the latest. If you have not received it by that date, ask your employer.

Share schemes and share benefits
If you have had any shares from an employee share scheme (whether approved or unapproved) you will have some correspondence from your employer. If you have exercised any option you should have a copy of the 'exercise note'. This happens when you actually buy some shares under the scheme at a price which has been fixed by the scheme.

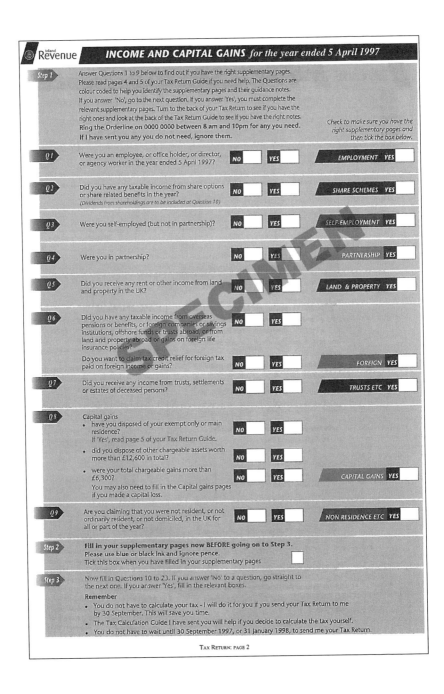

Fig. 3. Tax return page 2.

You may also receive shares either free or at a reduced price as part of your pay.

In all cases involving shares, you will need a note of the dates involved and the market prices of the shares at those dates. The company involved will be able to give you this information.

Self employment

You need the annual accounts, prepared up to the normal accounting date. Chapter 2 explained about keeping records from which to prepare the figures. Figure 4 shows the detail needed for income and expenses.

You also need details of capital equipment you bought or sold, and details of any Enterprise Allowance you received.

Partnership income

If you were in a business partnership, you need the partnership tax reference, and the amount of your share of the partnership profits for the year, including different types of partnership income (if any).

The person responsible for the tax affairs of the partnership will have had a tax return for the partnership, to declare the partnership income of different sorts. The total partnership income is then divided between the partners on the partnership return. You should therefore have a copy of those entries for your own purposes.

Warning

In the past you may have claimed expenses on your own tax return to claim against partnership profits. These expenses now must be claimed on the partnership tax return.

Property income

You need the records of the rents or other income due and received, records of the allowable expenses, and for certain types of income, records of capital equipment bought or sold.

Foreign income

For any income received from abroad, you need details of the gross amounts of income, the country it came from, and details of the foreign tax (if any) and the UK tax (if any). This applies to all forms of income from abroad – such as pensions, investments, rents, *etc.* You might therefore need bank statements for overseas accounts, receipts for foreign tax paid, *etc.*

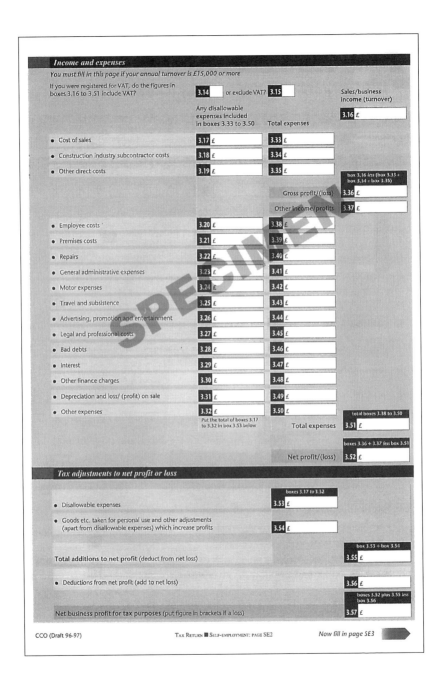

Income and expenses

You must fill in this page if your annual turnover is £15,000 or more

If you were registered for VAT, do the figures in boxes 3.16 to 3.51 include VAT? **3.14** [ ] or exclude VAT? **3.15** [ ]

Sales/business income (turnover)

3.16 £

	Any disallowable expenses included in boxes 3.33 to 3.50	Total expenses	
• Cost of sales	**3.17** £	**3.33** £	
• Construction industry subcontractor costs	**3.18** £	**3.34** £	
• Other direct costs	**3.19** £	**3.35** £	

box 3.16 less (box 3.33 + box 3.34 + box 3.35)

Gross profit/(loss) **3.36** £

Other income/profits **3.37** £

• Employee costs	**3.20** £	**3.38** £	
• Premises costs	**3.21** £	**3.39** £	
• Repairs	**3.22** £	**3.40** £	
• General administrative expenses	**3.23** £	**3.41** £	
• Motor expenses	**3.24** £	**3.42** £	
• Travel and subsistence	**3.25** £	**3.43** £	
• Advertising, promotion and entertainment	**3.26** £	**3.44** £	
• Legal and professional costs	**3.27** £	**3.45** £	
• Bad debts	**3.28** £	**3.46** £	
• Interest	**3.29** £	**3.47** £	
• Other finance charges	**3.30** £	**3.48** £	
• Depreciation and loss/ (profit) on sale	**3.31** £	**3.49** £	
• Other expenses	**3.32** £	**3.50** £	

Put the total of boxes 3.17 to 3.32 in box 3.53 below

total boxes 3.38 to 3.50

Total expenses **3.51** £

boxes 3.36 + 3.37 less box 3.51

Net profit/(loss) **3.52** £

Tax adjustments to net profit or loss

boxes 3.17 to 3.32

• Disallowable expenses **3.53** £

• Goods etc. taken for personal use and other adjustments (apart from disallowable expenses) which increase profits **3.54** £

box 3.53 + box 3.54

Total additions to net profit (deduct from net loss) **3.55** £

• Deductions from net profit (add to net loss) **3.56** £

boxes 3.52 plus 3.55 less box 3.56

Net business profit for tax purposes (put figure in brackets if a loss) **3.57** £

Fig. 4. Self employment page 2.

Income from trusts and settlements
You should receive a form R185 for any income you receive from trusts or estates of deceased persons. If you do not receive this form, ask the trustee for it.

Capital gains
You need:
- details of all assets you have sold or disposed of
- details of the original purchase by you of that asset – date and amount
- details of the indexation allowance available.

Non-resident claims
For this section you need details of your nationality, and dates of your movements between various countries during the tax year.

UK savings and investment income
Page 3 of the tax form is devoted to income from UK savings and investments. You must sort your information into the different categories. These include:

- interest from banks and building societies
- interest from unit trusts
- interest from First Option Bonds
- interest from other National Savings
- any other interest
- dividends from UK companies
- dividends from UK unit trusts
- stock dividends (also known as scrip dividends)
- foreign income dividends from UK companies
- foreign income dividends from UK unit trusts
- non qualifying distributions.

So, if you have interest from say two different building societies, and a bank, and a few shares and unit trusts, your list of items might be like Figure 5.

Warning
Although the amounts to enter in the boxes are in pounds only, include the amounts in pounds and pence in your lists.

Tip: Always round down to the nearest pound.

Interest from banks and building societies

	Gross	Tax	Net
Halifax Building Society	100.50	20.10	80.40
Woolwich Building Society	50.75	10.15	40.60
Lloyds Bank	200.60	40.12	160.48
	351.85	70.37	281.48

Dividends received from companies

	Dividend	Tax credit
British Telecom	80.50	16.10
GEC	120.60	24.12
Shell Transport & Trading	150.00	30.00
	351.10	70.22

Dividends received from unit trusts

	Dividend	Tax credit
Gartmore UT	100.50	20.10
Save and Prosper UT	150.40	30.08
	250.90	50.18

Fig. 5. Schedule of interest and dividends.

Pensions and Social Security benefits

You should keep details of your state pension. Do not throw away the order book when it is finished. The front cover includes details of the weekly amount. For other Social Security benefits, there may be similar order books. Keep the detail of the weekly amounts. In other cases, there will be some correspondence from the DSS telling you the amounts. You then need to work out the number of weeks you have been receiving the benefits.

> **Tip**: The extra 'Christmas bonus' paid to pensioners is **not** taxable. Do not add this in.

Example
You started to receive the state pension on 5 July at £64 per week. You therefore received 39 weeks during the tax year and the amount to enter is £2,496.

What if I have received a benefit which is not shown on the tax form?

Some benefits are not taxable, and do not need to be entered. If your benefit is not shown on the tax form, you do not need to declare it.

Other pensions
The next boxes are for you to enter any other pensions from the UK. These details are on the P60 which you should have received from your pension provider. If you do not receive a P60 soon after 5 April, ask your pension provider for one.

Any other income
On the same page, and covered by questions 12 and 13, are the boxes for any other income. Question 12 deals with:

1. Taxable maintenance or alimony received.
2. Gains on UK life assurance policies.
3. Deficiency relief on the above.
4. Refunds of surplus additional voluntary contributions on pensions.

If you have received any income under these headings, you should have received also some form of documentary evidence. Keep these to enable you to work out the figures.

Question 13 is for any other income of any sort not declared elsewhere. If there is anything at all not under any of the other categories, it is entered here.

Claiming reliefs

Page 5 deals with your claims for reliefs. You need details of amounts you have paid under the following headings:

- retirement annuity premiums
- personal pension premiums
- vocational training
- interest on loans for house purchase
- interest on other qualifying loans
- maintenance or alimony payments
- subscriptions to venture capital trusts
- subscriptions to enterprise investment schemes
- charitable covenants
- Gift Aid payments
- post cessation expenses
- losses on relevant discounted securities
- payments to a Trade Union or Friendly Society for death benefits.

Claiming allowances

Page 6 deals with the personal allowances you can claim.

If you claim the Blind Person's Allowance, you need details of the local authority under which you are registered.

If you claim the Additional Personal Allowance, you need details of the child you claim for, and his or her education if over age 16.

FILLING IN THE BOXES

Once you have all the information to hand, you can then go through the form and fill in all the boxes. Work through it methodically, following the steps shown on the form, and do not try to fill in any part out of sequence. It is important to fill in the boxes in the correct order.

Reading the notes

The first page of the return form consists of important notes. It tells you when you should get the return back to the Inspector of Taxes, and warns about penalties for late filing or for giving false

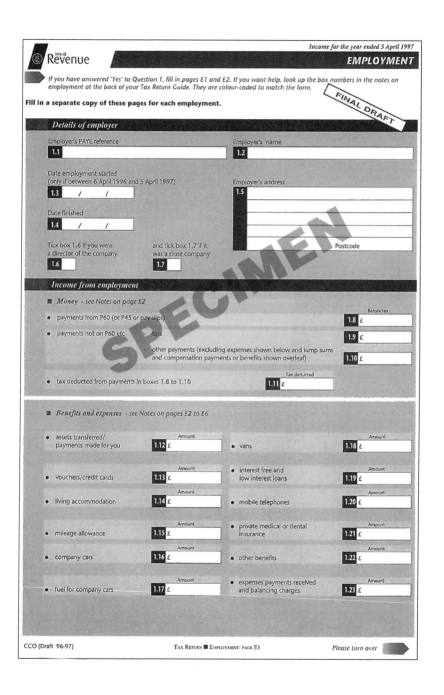

Income for the year ended 5 April 1997

Inland Revenue

EMPLOYMENT

If you have answered 'Yes' to Question 1, fill in pages E1 and E2. If you want help, look up the box numbers in the notes on employment at the back of your Tax Return Guide. They are colour-coded to match the form.

Fill in a separate copy of these pages for each employment.

Details of employer

Employer's PAYE reference
1.1

Employer's name
1.2

Date employment started
(only if between 6 April 1996 and 5 April 1997)
1.3 / /

Date finished
1.4 / /

Employer's address
1.5

Postcode

Tick box 1.6 if you were a director of the company **1.6**

and tick box 1.7 if it was a close company **1.7**

Income from employment

■ **Money** - see Notes on page E2

- payments from P60 (or P45 or pay slips) — Before tax **1.8** £
- payments not on P60 etc — tips **1.9** £
- other payments (excluding expenses shown below and lump sums and compensation payments or benefits shown overleaf) **1.10** £
- tax deducted from payments in boxes 1.8 to 1.10 — Tax deducted **1.11** £

■ **Benefits and expenses** - see Notes on pages E2 to E6

- assets transferred/ payments made for you — Amount **1.12** £
- vans — Amount **1.18** £
- vouchers/credit cards — Amount **1.13** £
- interest free and low interest loans — Amount **1.19** £
- living accommodation — Amount **1.14** £
- mobile telephones — Amount **1.20** £
- mileage allowance — Amount **1.15** £
- private medical or dental insurance — Amount **1.21** £
- company cars — Amount **1.16** £
- other benefits — Amount **1.22** £
- fuel for company cars — Amount **1.17** £
- expenses payments received and balancing charges — Amount **1.23** £

CCO (Draft 96-97)   TAX RETURN ■ EMPLOYMENT: PAGE E1   Please turn over ➤

Fig. 6 Employment page 1.

43

Income from employment continued

■ *Lump sums and compensation payments or benefits*

You must read the notes on page E6 and fill in Help Sheet IR204 ***before*** *filling in boxes 1.24 to 1.30*

Reliefs

- £30,000 exemption — 1.24 £
- foreign service and disability — 1.25 £
- retirement and death lump sums — 1.26 £

Taxable lump sums

- from working sheet, box H (from Help Sheet IR204) — 1.27 £
- from working sheet, box Q (from Help Sheet IR204) — 1.28 £
- from working sheet, box R (from Help Sheet IR204) — 1.29 £
- tax deducted from payments in boxes 1.27 to 1.29 — Tax deducted 1.30 £

■ *Foreign earnings not taxable in the UK in year ended 5 April 1997* - *see Notes on page E6* — 1.31 £

■ *Expenses you incurred in doing your job* - *see Notes on page E6*

- travel and subsistence costs — 1.32 £
- fixed deductions for expenses — 1.33 £
- professional fees and subscriptions — 1.34 £
- other expenses and capital allowances — 1.35 £
- tick box 1.36 if the figure in box 1.32 includes travelling from home to work — 1.36

■ *Foreign Earnings Deduction* — 1.37 £

■ *Foreign tax for which tax credit relief not claimed* — 1.38 £

Additional information

Now fill in any other supplementary pages that apply to you.
Otherwise, go back to page 3 in your Tax Return and finish filling it in.

CCO (Draft 96-97) TAX RETURN ■ EMPLOYMENT: PAGE E2

Fig. 7. Employment page 2.

information. It also gives a telephone number for a helpline, and directs you to where you may get help from the Inland Revenue.

Step 1
This consists of filling in the first nine questions on page 2. They are all 'Yes' or 'No' answers. (See Figure 2 earlier in this chapter.)

Step 2
This directs you to the supplementary pages for which you answered 'Yes' in step 1. You should go through these in order. Each supplementary page comes with a set of notes to help you fill them in. The notes also give a list of help sheets on various topics, and you may need these if you have any items to which they refer.

Employment
Figure 6 shows the first page of this section.

You need a separate form for each employment during the tax year. If you had several employments you may need to ask for more forms. Boxes 1.1 to 1.5 are for details of your employer, and the date you started or finished work, if it was in the tax year. Tick box 1.6 if you were a director, and 1.7 if the company was a close company. This means a company with five or fewer shareholders, or a company in which the only shareholders are also directors.

Fill in the details from your P60 in box 1.8 and 1.11 showing total taxable earnings and the tax deducted. Then fill in any amounts not on your P60, such as tips, in boxes 1.9 and 1.10.

Next, fill in the details in boxes 1.12 to 1.23 of any benefits or expenses reimbursed. These figures all come from the P11D which your employer would have given you if you had any benefits.

Figure 7 shows the second page of this section. This deals with reliefs, taxable lumps sums, foreign earnings and expenses claimed. If you have any items to declare in boxes 1.24 to 1.29, you should have help sheet IR 204. This tells you what to declare from lump sums, and claims for relief for foreign service.

Box 3.1 deals with foreign earnings. If you claim for non-resident status, or have earnings in a foreign country which you cannot bring into this country, help sheet IR 211 shows you how to arrive at the figure you enter here.

Claiming expenses
Boxes 1.32 to 1.36 are for claiming expenses incurred in doing your job. You may claim the following expenses:

Capital allowances claimed for car – 50% private use

		Claim
Cost of car – year 1	14,000	
Capital allowance year 1 – limited	3,000	1,500
	11,000	
Year 2 Capital allowances	2,750	1,375
	8,250	
Year 3	2,062	1,031
	6,188	

etc.

Fig. 8. Capital allowance claim.

1996/97 mileage rates	First 4,000 miles	Excess over 4,000 miles
Engine size:		
Up to 1,000 c.c.	27p	16p
1,001 – 1,500 c.c.	34p	19p
1,501 – 2,000 c.c.	43p	23p
Over 2,000 c.c.	61p	33p

Fig. 9. Fixed profit car scheme.

		Box
1.	Necessary travelling expenses and related meal and accommodation costs incurred in doing your job	1.32
2.	Other necessary expenses incurred solely in doing your job	1.33 to 1.35

Travelling

Travelling expenses may be in this country or abroad, and they may be for fares or motoring expenses. The only qualification is that they must be for business travel.

Travelling from your home to your normal place of work is *always* private. You cannot claim for it. If there is any element of travel from home to work included in box 1.32, then you must tick box 1.36.

Motoring

If you claim motoring expenses, you may claim on an exact basis, or on the simpler 'fixed profit car scheme'.

The exact basis means that you must keep a record of all your journeys, and the total mileage of the tax year is divided between business and private mileage. Then the total costs of the car are divided between the business and the private part, and the business part is claimable. You may also claim the same proportion of **capital allowances** on the cost of the car under this basis.

Capital allowances are tax allowances on the cost of the car to spread the cost of buying it over its life. This is done by allowing 25 per cent of the cost as an allowance in the first year, then deducting that, and allowing 25 per cent of the remaining balance in the next year, and so on. There is a maximum claim of £3,000 in any one tax year. Figure 8 shows how this works.

The simpler method is to use the 'fixed profit car scheme' figures of a mileage allowance for the total number of business miles. You must also keep mileage records to claim this method. The amount you can claim for 1996/97 is shown in Figure 9.

Fixed deductions

Some employments have fixed deductions agreed between the Inland Revenue and Trade Unions or other bodies. If your employment is covered by any such agreement, enter your figure in box 1.33.

Professional fees and subscriptions
Certain jobs, mainly in the professions, require fees or subscriptions to professional bodies to enable you to work in that profession. These are claimable. If you are in any doubt, ask the body to which you pay. The amount is entered in box 1.34.

Other expenses
Any other items you pay in the performance of your job may be claimable. This could include things such as tools or equipment you are required to provide for your job. If you are in any doubt, ask your tax adviser or the Inspector of Taxes. These go in box 1.35.

Tip: Do not always accept the first answer you are given by the Inspector of Taxes. If you believe you have a good case, and it is not accepted at first, be prepared to argue your case.

Capital allowances
In the same way that capital allowances may be claimed on cars as described above, they may also be claimed on other equipment or machinery that you have to supply to do your job. These are also included in box 1.35.

Foreign earnings deduction
If you worked part of the year abroad, and you are claiming non-resident status, then you may be able to claim a deduction for the part of your earnings which relate to your work abroad. It all depends on whether you had enough days out of the country. Help sheet IR 205 gives you a work sheet to calculate if you are due for a deduction under this scheme. If so, enter it in box 1.37.

Foreign tax
If you have suffered foreign tax, you may be able to claim a credit. If this is your case, you must get the foreign supplementary sheets and notes. The working sheet in the notes tells you how to work this out. If you do not wish to claim this, then you enter the foreign tax paid in box 1.38.

Share schemes
Figure 10 shows the first page of the share schemes pages.
　　This section deals with options given by companies for their

Income for the year ended 5 April 1997

Inland Revenue

SHARE SCHEMES

If you have answered 'Yes' to Question 2, fill in pages S1 and S2. If you want help, look up the box numbers in the notes on share schemes at the back of your Tax Return Guide. They are colour-coded to match the form.

FINAL DRAFT

SPECIMEN

Share options

*Read the notes on pages S1 to S4 **before** filling in the boxes*

■ *Approved savings-related share options*

	Name of company	Tick if shares unquoted	Taxable amount
• Exercise	2.1	2.2	2.3 £
• Cancellation or release	2.4	2.5	2.6 £

■ *Approved discretionary share options*

	Name of company		
• Exercise	2.7	2.8	2.9 £
• Cancellation or release	2.10	2.11	2.12 £

■ *Unapproved share options*

	Name of company		
• Grant	2.13	2.14	2.15 £
• Exercise	2.16	2.17	2.18 £
• Cancellation or release	2.19	2.20	2.21 £

Shares acquired

*Read the notes on page S5 **before** filling in the boxes*

	Name of company		
• Shares received from your employment	2.22	2.23	2.24 £
• Shares as benefit	2.25	2.26	2.27 £
• Post acquisition charges	2.28	2.29	2.30 £

Total taxable amount — total column above 2.31 £

Additional information

CCO (Draft 96-97) — Tax Return ■ Share schemes: page S1

Fig. 10. Share schemes p.1.

You must complete a separate copy of this page for each taxable event in the year ended 5 April 1997 which relates to your share options or shares acquired. If you had more than one taxable event in the year, either photocopy this page or ask the Orderline for more copies.

Share options

Read the notes on pages S2 to S4 before filling in the boxes

Name of company
2.32

Class of share (for example, 10p Ordinary)
2.33

	Grant	Exercise	Cancellation/Release
2.34 Date option was granted	/ /	/ /	/ /
2.35 Date option was exercised		/ /	
2.36 Number of shares			
2.37 Exercise price/option price per share	£ .	£ .	
2.38 Amount paid for option	£ .	£ .	£ .
2.39 Market value per share at date the option was granted	£ .		
2.40 Market value per share at date the option was exercised		£ .	
2.41 Amount received in money or money's worth			£ .

Shares acquired

Read the notes on page S5 before filling in the boxes

Name of company
2.42

Class of share (for example, 10p Ordinary)
2.43

	Shares acquired	Post acquisition charge
2.44 Date shares acquired	/ /	/ /
2.45 Number of shares		
2.46 Amount paid per share	£ .	
2.47 Market value per share at date of acquisition	£ .	£ .
2.48 Give details of the nature of the post acquisition event		

SPECIMEN

Fig. 11. Share schemes p. 2.

employees or their directors to buy shares in the company at advantageous prices. There are three stages to a share option:

1. The grant of the option: this happens when the company issues you with a certificate stating that you are entitled to buy its shares at given dates at a certain price.

2. The exercise of the option: this happens when you actually buy the shares at the special price.

3. The cancellation or release of the option: this happens when, for whatever reason, the company pays you an inducement to give up your option, or not to exercise it.

There are three types of share option schemes:

1. Approved savings-related schemes: this is when the option is granted in connection with a savings scheme by which you make regular savings into a company account, and the shares are bought out of this savings account.

2. Approved discretionary share option schemes: this is when the company grants options on its own discretion, and is often for directors or other executives.

3. Unapproved share option schemes: these do not have any Inland Revenue approval, so do not benefit from favourable tax treatment.

The work sheets on the notes provide all the calculations needed to cover the different stages, and give you the amount to enter on the supplementary sheets.

If you are in an **approved share option scheme**, fill in boxes 2.1 to 2.6 for any options you exercised or any that were cancelled or released.

If you are in an **approved discretionary share option scheme**, fill in the boxes 2.7 to 2.12 for any options you exercised or any that were cancelled or released.

If you are in any **unapproved share option schemes**, fill in boxes 2.13 to 2.21 for any grants of options, any options exercised, or any cancelled or released.

If you received any **shares free or cheaply**, the taxable amounts are calculated on working sheet 6 of the notes pages, and entered in boxes 2.22 to 2.30.

The total of all the taxable amounts is then added up and entered in box 2.31.

Figure 11 shows the second page of his section. It is for the details of the company and the dates, and amounts of the share options. A separate copy of this page is required for each taxable event. You may photocopy this page for that purpose, or ask for more copies.

Self employment

Figure 12 shows the first page of this section.

This page is for the name and address of the business, and the type of business, and the accounting period dates – boxes 3.1 to 3.8.

If the total turnover of the business is less than £15,000, you need only enter three figures – total turnover, expenses, and net profit in boxes 3.11 to 3.13.

Profits

Figure 4 earlier in this chapter showed the next page of this section.

If the turnover is £15,000 or more, enter the **sales** and detailed **expenses** on this page.

Also identify any disallowable expenses (such as entertaining *etc*) which are then shown as an adjustment to the net profit figure. Other adjustments are also shown, including goods *etc* taken for personal use, and deduction of items which may be included in turnover, but are not taxable (such as bank interest already taxed).

Boxes 3.14 to 3.15 are for you to declare if you are **VAT registered** and if the figures are inclusive or exclusive of VAT.

The total turnover is shown in box 3.16.

Expenses are shown in boxes 3.17 to 3.50, with the left-hand column showing disallowable expenses.

The expenses are totalled in box 3.51, then deducted from the turnover to give the profit figure which goes in box 3.52.

Adjustments are then made for disallowable expenses. The totals of all the left-hand column's figures are totalled in box 3.53. Goods taken from the business for private use are entered in box 3.54, and boxes 3.53 and 3.54 totalled in box 3.55. This is then added to the profit figure, and any adjustments which would reduce the profit are entered in box 3.56 and the final adjusted profit entered in box 3.57.

Capital allowances

Figure 13 shows page 3 of the self employed section.

Boxes 3.58 to 3.67 are for claiming capital allowances. These are calculated in the same way as illustrated above in Figure 8. Capital allowance claims may be made on:

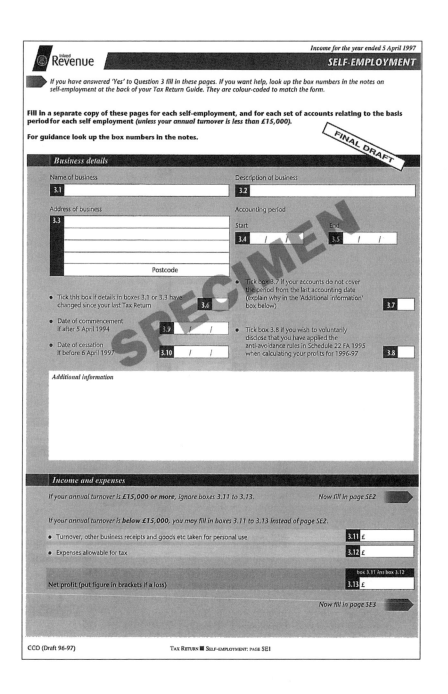

Income for the year ended 5 April 1997

Revenue
Inland

SELF-EMPLOYMENT

If you have answered 'Yes' to Question 3 fill in these pages. If you want help, look up the box numbers in the notes on self-employment at the back of your Tax Return Guide. They are colour-coded to match the form.

Fill in a separate copy of these pages for each self-employment, and for each set of accounts relating to the basis period for each self employment *(unless your annual turnover is less than £15,000).*

For guidance look up the box numbers in the notes.

FINAL DRAFT

Business details

Name of business

3.1

Description of business

3.2

Address of business

3.3

Postcode

Accounting period

Start

3.4 / /

End

3.5 / /

- Tick this box if details in boxes 3.1 or 3.3 have changed since your last Tax Return

3.6

- Date of commencement if after 5 April 1994

3.9 / /

- Date of cessation if before 6 April 1997

3.10 / /

- Tick box 3.7 if your accounts do not cover the period from the last accounting date (explain why in the 'Additional information' box below)

3.7

- Tick box 3.8 if you wish to voluntarily disclose that you have applied the anti-avoidance rules in Schedule 22 FA 1995 when calculating your profits for 1996-97

3.8

Additional information

Income and expenses

If your annual turnover is £15,000 or more, ignore boxes 3.11 to 3.13.

Now fill in page SE2

If your annual turnover is below £15,000, you may fill in boxes 3.11 to 3.13 instead of page SE2.

- Turnover, other business receipts and goods etc taken for personal use

3.11 £

- Expenses allowable for tax

3.12 £

box 3.11 *less* box 3.12

Net profit (put figure in brackets if a loss)

3.13 £

Now fill in page SE3

CCO (Draft 96-97)   TAX RETURN ■ SELF-EMPLOYMENT: PAGE SE1

Fig. 12. Self employment page 1.

53

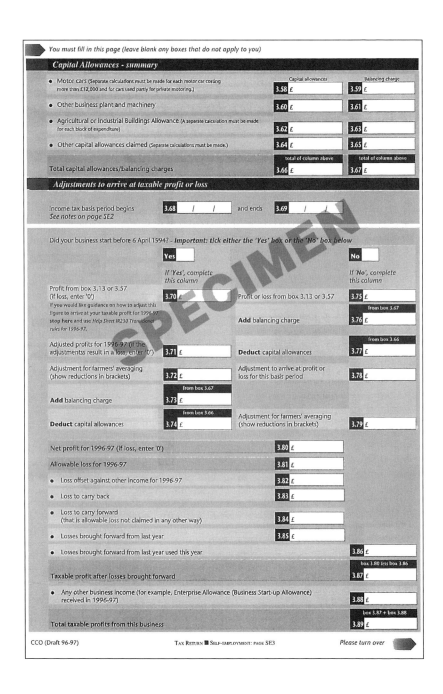

You must fill in this page (leave blank any boxes that do not apply to you)

Capital Allowances - summary

	Capital allowances	Balancing charge
• Motor cars (Separate calculations must be made for each motor car costing more than £12,000 and for cars used partly for private motoring.)	3.58 £	3.59 £
• Other business plant and machinery	3.60 £	3.61 £
• Agricultural or Industrial Buildings Allowance (A separate calculation must be made for each block of expenditure)	3.62 £	3.63 £
• Other capital allowances claimed (Separate calculations must be made.)	3.64 £	3.65 £
	total of column above	total of column above
Total capital allowances/balancing charges	3.66 £	3.67 £

Adjustments to arrive at taxable profit or loss

Income tax basis period begins   3.68 / /   and ends   3.69 / /
See notes on page SE2

Did your business start before 6 April 1994? - **Important: tick either the 'Yes' box or the 'No' box below**

Yes   No

If 'Yes', complete this column	If 'No', complete this column
Profit from box 3.13 or 3.57 (if loss, enter '0') **3.70** £	Profit or loss from box 3.13 or 3.57 **3.75** £
If you would like guidance on how to adjust this figure to arrive at your taxable profit for 1996-97 **stop here** and use *Help Sheet IR230 Transitional rules for 1996-97.*	from box 3.67 **Add** balancing charge **3.76** £
Adjusted profits for 1996-97 (if the adjustmentss result in a loss, enter '0') **3.71** £	from box 3.66 **Deduct** capital allowances **3.77** £
Adjustment for farmers' averaging (show reductions in brackets) **3.72** £	Adjustment to arrive at profit or loss for this basis period **3.78** £
from box 3.67 **Add** balancing charge **3.73** £	
from box 3.66 **Deduct** capital allowances **3.74** £	Adjustment for farmers' averaging (show reductions in brackets) **3.79** £

Net profit for 1996-97 (if loss, enter '0')	3.80 £
Allowable loss for 1996-97	3.81 £
• Loss offset against other income for 1996-97	3.82 £
• Loss to carry back	3.83 £
• Loss to carry forward (that is allowable loss not claimed in any other way)	3.84 £
• Losses brought forward from last year	3.85 £
• Losses brought forward from last year used this year	3.86 £
	box 3.80 less box 3.86
Taxable profit after losses brought forward	3.87 £
• Any other business income (for example, Enterprise Allowance (Business Start-up Allowance) received in 1996-97)	3.88 £
	box 3.87 + box 3.88
Total taxable profits from this business	3.89 £

Fig. 13. Self employment page 3.

- motors cars
- other vehicles
- plant and equipment (including machinery)
- agricultural buildings
- industrial buildings
- cemeteries and crematoria
- dredging
- dwelling houses let on assured tenancies
- patent rights
- scientific research.

Each of these have their own rules, and capital allowances are claimed and entered on this section. Capital allowances may be disclaimed, or claimed in part. A later chapter will look at this in more detail.

Adjustments and tax losses

Boxes 3.68 to 3.89 are for various adjustments, which may be due to the change to the current year basis of assessment or due to special adjustments for certain types of business, such as farmers. The help sheets explain how these adjustments are to be entered.

Boxes 3.68 to 3.69 are for the beginning and end dates of the **accounting period**.

Then, you decide which set of boxes to fill in, depending on whether your business started before or after 6 April 1994. If it started before, there are special transitional rules for the 1996/97 tax year only, and help sheet IR 230 shows you how to arrive at the figure to put in box 3.71. If your business started after 6 April 1994, then you enter the figure of profit from box 3.13 (if your turnover was under £15,000) or box 3.57.

Adjustments are then made for capital allowances, and special claims. The taxable profit is put in box 3.80, or loss in box 3.81.

Losses are dealt with in boxes 3.82 to 3.85. You may choose the way in which you would like your losses to be dealt with. These are also shown in help sheet IR 227, with a work sheet for allocating losses. They can be:

- offset against other income of the same year
- carried back to earlier years and offset (if the loss was made in the early years of a new business)
- carried forward to offset against future years' profits.

When losses have been adjusted against profits, any other business

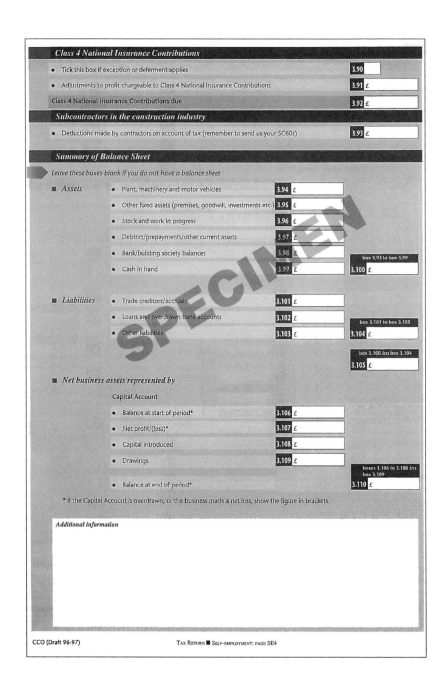

Class 4 National Insurance Contributions

- Tick this box if exception or deferment applies — 3.90
- Adjustments to profit chargeable to Class 4 National Insurance Contributions — 3.91 £
- Class 4 National Insurance Contributions due — 3.92 £

Subcontractors in the construction industry

- Deductions made by contractors on account of tax (remember to send us your SC60s) — 3.93 £

Summary of Balance Sheet

Leave these boxes blank if you do not have a balance sheet

- **Assets**
  - Plant, machinery and motor vehicles — 3.94 £
  - Other fixed assets (premises, goodwill, investments etc.) — 3.95 £
  - Stock and work in progress — 3.96 £
  - Debtors/prepayments/other current assets — 3.97 £
  - Bank/building society balances — 3.98 £
  - Cash in hand — 3.99 £

  box 3.94 to box 3.99 — 3.100 £

- **Liabilities**
  - Trade creditors/accruals — 3.101 £
  - Loans and overdrawn bank accounts — 3.102 £
  - Other liabilities — 3.103 £

  box 3.101 to box 3.103 — 3.104 £

  box 3.100 less box 3.104 — 3.105 £

- **Net business assets represented by**

  Capital Account
  - Balance at start of period* — 3.106 £
  - Net profit/(loss)* — 3.107 £
  - Capital introduced — 3.108 £
  - Drawings — 3.109 £

  boxes 3.106 to 3.108 less box 3.109 — 3.110 £

  - Balance at end of period* — 3.110 £

  * If the Capital Account is overdrawn, or the business made a net loss, show the figure in brackets.

Additional information

Fig. 14. Self employment page 4.

income (such as Enterprise Allowance) is added in box 3.88 to arrive at a final taxable figure in box 3.89.

Figure 14 shows page 4 of this section.

Class 4 National Insurance

If there are any adjustments to profits for Class 4 National Insurance purposes, or exemption from Class 4 due to age, they are shown in boxes 3.90 to 3.92. The work sheet on page SE 7 of the notes shows how to work out the actual Class 4 contributions which goes in box 3.92.

Subcontractors in the construction industry

If you are a subcontractor and you have had tax deducted, enter it in box 3.93, and attach your SC60 certificate.

Balance sheet

If you have accounts with a balance sheet, you must summarise it in boxes 3.94 to 3.110. If you do not have a balance sheet, you do not have to fill in this part of this section.

Partnerships

There are two types of supplementary sheets for partners in businesses. The short version is issued when it is believed that the partnership income consists only of trading income and taxed interest.

If you are a member of more than one business partnership, you should have a return for each partnership.

Figure 15 shows the first page of the **short version**. Fill in boxes 4.1 to 4.4 to show the partnership details, and the dates you started or ceased being a partner, if during the tax year. Boxes 4.5 to 4.6 are for the dates of the partnership basis period. This applies if the partnership started before 6 April 1994. Box 4.7 is for your share of the partnership profit for the tax year. Boxes 4.8 to 4.19 are for adjustments, losses *etc* in the same way as the boxes 3.70 to 3.89 on the self employment pages.

Boxes 4.20 to 4.22 are for the Class 4 National Insurance figures, and are worked out in the same way as the boxes 3.90 to 3.92 on the self employment pages.

Figure 16 shows page 2 of this part. On this page show your share of:

• partnership taxed income (such as bank interest) in box 4.65

- other partnership income in box 4.68
- income tax paid in box 4.69
- SC60 deductions in box 4.70.

Boxes 4.69 and 4.70 are totalled to box 4.72.

If the partnership started before 6 April 1994, your share of the tax assessed for 1996/97 goes in box 4.74 and your share of the Class 4 National Insurance in box 4.75.

The **full version** covers all possible types of partnership income. Page 1 is exactly the same as page 1 of the short version.

Figures 17 and 18 show pages 2 and 3.

Boxes 4.23 and 4.24 are for the dates of the basis period. Other boxes are for:

- UK savings income (boxes 4.25 to 4.27)
- foreign savings income (boxes 4.28 to 4.32)
- untaxed other UK income (boxes 4.33 to 4.39)
- untaxed other foreign income (boxes 4.40 to 4.47)
- income from offshore funds (boxes 4.48 to 4.51)
- income from UK land and property (boxes 4.52 to 4.56 and 4.57 to 4.62)
- taxed savings income (boxes 4.63 to 4.68)
- tax credits (boxes 4.69 to 4.73).

Boxes 4.74 and 4.75 are the same as the short version.

Income from land and property

Figure 19 shows page 1 of the land and property section.

If you are claiming Rent a Room relief, and the rents you receive are £3,250 or less, all you need to do is tick the 'yes' box on question 1, and you are finished with this section.

Rent a Room

This applies when you provide accommodation in your home (apart from a guest house or bed and breakfast business).

The Rent a Room scheme means that the first £3,250 (for 1996/97) of the income you receive is tax free, and you are only taxed on any rent above £3,250. The limit of £3,250 is per household, not per person. Therefore, if you share a house, and more than one person lets out a part of the house, the £3,250 limit is shared between them.

You may calculate the actual income less expenses. This may be useful if you have made a loss, since the loss would then be claimable against other property income of the same year. If there is no other property income of the same year, the loss may be carried forward to offset against future income.

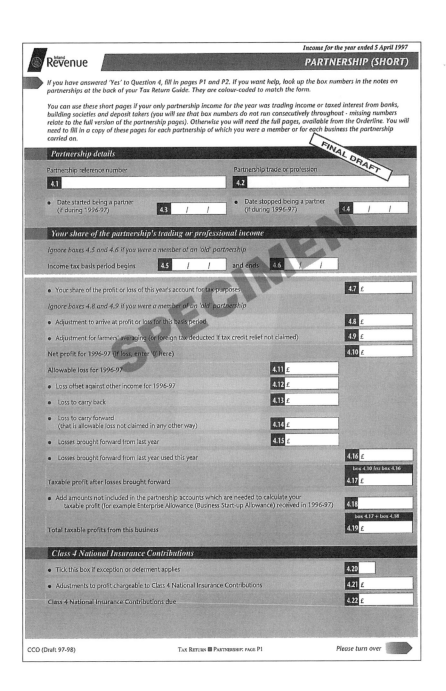

Inland Revenue

PARTNERSHIP (SHORT)

If you have answered 'Yes' to Question 4, fill in pages P1 and P2. If you want help, look up the box numbers in the notes on partnerships at the back of your Tax Return Guide. They are colour-coded to match the form.

You can use these short pages if your only partnership income for the year was trading income or taxed interest from banks, building societies and deposit takers (you will see that box numbers do not run consecutively throughout - missing numbers relate to the full version of the partnership pages). Otherwise you will need the full pages, available from the Orderline. You will need to fill in a copy of these pages for each partnership of which you were a member or for each business the partnership carried on.

FINAL DRAFT

Partnership details

Partnership reference number

4.1

Partnership trade or profession

4.2

- Date started being a partner (if during 1996-97) **4.3** / /

- Date stopped being a partner (if during 1996-97) **4.4** / /

Your share of the partnership's trading or professional income

Ignore boxes 4.5 and 4.6 if you were a member of an 'old' partnership

Income tax basis period begins **4.5** / / and ends **4.6** / /

- Your share of the profit or loss of this year's account for tax purposes **4.7** £

Ignore boxes 4.8 and 4.9 if you were a member of an 'old' partnership

- Adjustment to arrive at profit or loss for this basis period **4.8** £

- Adjustment for farmers' averaging (or foreign tax deducted if tax credit relief not claimed) **4.9** £

Net profit for 1996-97 (if loss, enter '0' here) **4.10** £

Allowable loss for 1996-97 **4.11** £

- Loss offset against other income for 1996-97 **4.12** £

- Loss to carry back **4.13** £

- Loss to carry forward (that is allowable loss not claimed in any other way) **4.14** £

- Losses brought forward from last year **4.15** £

- Losses brought forward from last year used this year **4.16** £

box 4.10 less box 4.16

Taxable profit after losses brought forward **4.17** £

- Add amounts not included in the partnership accounts which are needed to calculate your taxable profit (for example Enterprise Allowance (Business Start-up Allowance) received in 1996-97) **4.18**

box 4.17 + box 4.18

Total taxable profits from this business **4.19** £

Class 4 National Insurance Contributions

- Tick this box if exception or deferment applies **4.20**

- Adjustments to profit chargeable to Class 4 National Insurance Contributions **4.21** £

Class 4 National Insurance Contributions due **4.22** £

Fig. 15. Partnership (short version) page 1.

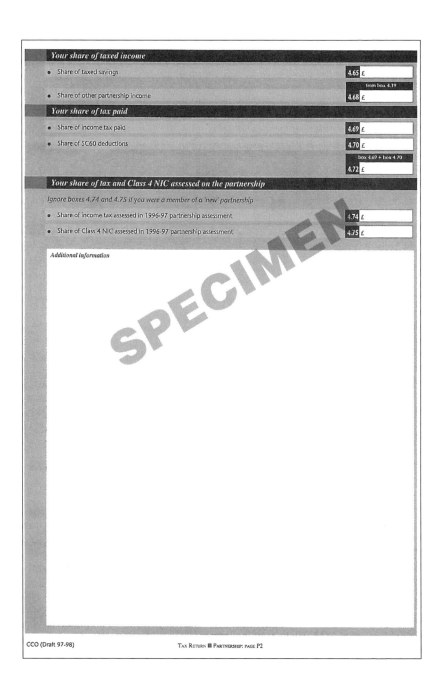

Your share of taxed income

- Share of taxed savings

4.65 £

from box 4.19

- Share of other partnership income

4.68 £

Your share of tax paid

- Share of income tax paid

4.69 £

- Share of SC60 deductions

4.70 £

box 4.69 + box 4.70

4.72 £

Your share of tax and Class 4 NIC assessed on the partnership

Ignore boxes 4.74 and 4.75 if you were a member of a 'new' partnership

- Share of income tax assessed in 1996-97 partnership assessment

4.74 £

- Share of Class 4 NIC assessed in 1996-97 partnership assessment

4.75 £

Additional information

SPECIMEN

Fig. 16. Partnership (short version) page 2.

Your share of untaxed income

Remember: the way in which you fill in pages P2 and P3 depends on whether you were a member of an 'old' partnership or a 'new' partnership.

Income tax basis period begins **4.23** / / and ends **4.24** / /

■ Income from UK savings

- Allocated share of savings **4.25** £
- Adjustment to profit **4.26** £   • Adjusted income for basis period **4.27** £

■ Income from foreign savings

- Allocated profit **4.28** £
- Adjustment to profit **4.29** £
- Total foreign tax deducted if tax credit relief not claimed **4.30** £   • Adjusted income for basis period **4.31** £

Untaxed income liable at 20%   box 4.27 + box 4.31 **4.32** £

■ Other untaxed UK income

- Allocated loss for 1996-97 **4.33** £   • Allocated profit **4.34** £
- Adjusted loss for basis period **4.35** £   • Adjusted profit **4.36** £
- Loss brought forward **4.37** £
- Loss carried forward **4.38** £

Taxable profit after adjustment and losses. Enter '0' if a loss **4.39** £

■ Other untaxed foreign income

- Allocated loss for 1996-97 **4.40** £   • Allocated profit **4.41** £
- Adjusted loss for basis period **4.42** £   • Adjusted profit **4.43** £
- Loss brought forward **4.44** £
- Total foreign tax deducted if tax credit relief not claimed **4.45** £
- Loss carried forward **4.46** £

Taxable profit after adjustment and losses. Enter '0' if a loss **4.47** £

■ Income from offshore funds

- Allocated profit **4.48** £
- Adjusted profit **4.49** £
- Total foreign tax deducted if tax credit relief not claimed **4.50** £

Taxable profit after adjustment **4.51** £

CCO (Draft 96-97)   TAX RETURN ■ PARTNERSHIP: PAGE P2

Fig. 17. Partnership (full version) page2.

61

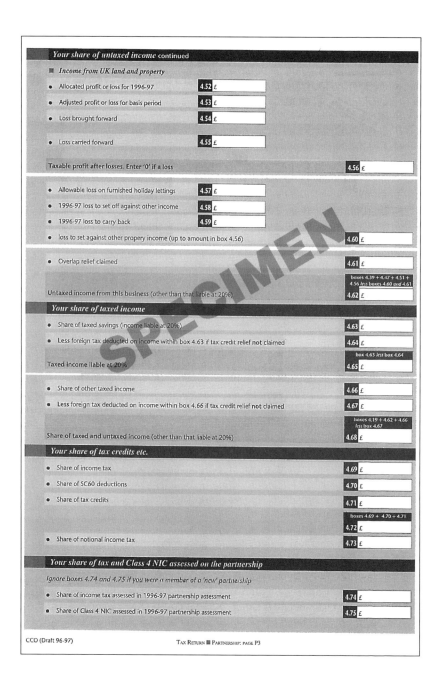

Your share of untaxed income continued

■ *Income from UK land and property*

- Allocated profit or loss for 1996-97 — **4.52** £
- Adjusted profit or loss for basis period — **4.53** £
- Loss brought forward — **4.54** £
- Loss carried forward — **4.55** £

Taxable profit after losses. Enter '0' if a loss — **4.56** £

- Allowable loss on furnished holiday lettings — **4.57** £
- 1996-97 loss to set off against other income — **4.58** £
- 1996-97 loss to carry back — **4.59** £
- loss to set against other propery income (up to amount in box 4.56) — **4.60** £
- Overlap relief claimed — **4.61** £

boxes 4.39 + 4.47 + 4.51 + 4.56 *less* boxes 4.60 *and* 4.61
Untaxed income from this business (other than that liable at 20%) — **4.62** £

Your share of taxed income

- Share of taxed savings (income liable at 20%) — **4.63** £
- **Less** foreign tax deducted on income within box 4.63 if tax credit relief **not** claimed — **4.64** £

box 4.63 *less* box 4.64
Taxed income liable at 20% — **4.65** £

- Share of other taxed income — **4.66** £
- **Less** foreign tax deducted on income within box 4.66 if tax credit relief **not** claimed — **4.67** £

boxes 4.19 + 4.62 + 4.66 *less* box 4.67
Share of taxed and untaxed income (other than that liable at 20%) — **4.68** £

Your share of tax credits etc.

- Share of income tax — **4.69** £
- Share of SC60 deductions — **4.70** £
- Share of tax credits — **4.71** £

boxes 4.69 + 4.70 + 4.71
4.72 £

- Share of notional income tax — **4.73** £

Your share of tax and Class 4 NIC assessed on the partnership

Ignore boxes 4.74 and 4.75 if you were a member of a 'new' partnership

- Share of income tax assessed in 1996-97 partnership assessment — **4.74** £
- Share of Class 4 NIC assessed in 1996-97 partnership assessment — **4.75** £

CCO (Draft 96-97)   TAX RETURN ■ PARTNERSHIP: PAGE P3

Fig. 18. Partnership (full version) page 3.

Furnished holiday lettings
Furnished holiday lettings are treated more advantageously than other property income. To qualify as a furnished holiday letting, the following conditions must be met:

(a) the property must actually be furnished
(b) it must be available as holiday letting to the public for at least 140 days during the year on a commercial basis
(c) it must actually be let commercially at least 70 days in the year
(d) it must not be let continuously to the same person for more than 31 days.

The total income from all furnished holiday lettings is shown in box 5.1, then expenses listed under the following headings:

- rent, rates, insurance and ground rents (box 5.2)
- repairs maintenance and renewals (box 5.3)
- finance charges and interest (box 5.4)
- legal and professional charges (box 5.5)
- cost of services provided, including wages (box 5.6)
- other expenses (box 5.7).

The expenses are totalled to box 5.8.

However, if the total income from holiday lettings is less than £15,000, you need only enter the total expenses in box 5.8.

Adjustments are then made for private use, and capital allowances (boxes 5.10 to 5.13). The resultant profit or loss goes in box 5.14 (profit) or 5.15 (loss).

If there is a loss, fill in boxes 5.16 to 5.18 to say whether you want the loss offset against other income of the same year, other property income of the same year, or carried back for relief in earlier years.

Other property income
Figure 20 shows page 2.

Enter income from other sorts of property here. The profit from furnished holiday letting is transferred to box 5.19 from 5.14. Rents and other income are entered in box 5.20. This is total income, so if there is income from various sources, you must add them up to get the total. Tax deducted is entered in box 5.21. Other income may consist of ground rents, tipping rights, wayleaves, sporting rights, *etc.*

If you receive premiums on a lease of up to 50 years, calculate these separately and enter in box 5.22. The work sheet on page L5 of the notes shows how to work out the figure.

Expenses are then detailed under the same headings as for

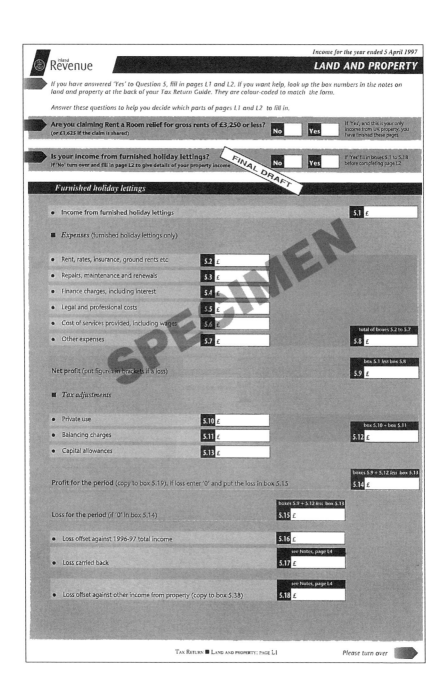

If you have answered 'Yes' to Question 5, fill in pages L1 and L2. If you want help, look up the box numbers in the notes on land and property at the back of your Tax Return Guide. They are colour-coded to match the form.

Answer these questions to help you decide which parts of pages L1 and L2 to fill in.

Are you claiming Rent a Room relief for gross rents of £3,250 or less? (or £1,625 if the claim is shared) — No / Yes — If 'Yes', and this is your only income from UK property, you have finished these pages

Is your income from furnished holiday lettings? If 'No' turn over and fill in page L2 to give details of your property income — No / Yes — If 'Yes' fill in boxes 5.1 to 5.18 before completing page L2

FINAL DRAFT

Furnished holiday lettings

- Income from furnished holiday lettings — 5.1 £

■ *Expenses* (furnished holiday lettings only)

- Rent, rates, insurance, ground rents etc — 5.2 £
- Repairs, maintenance and renewals — 5.3 £
- Finance charges, including interest — 5.4 £
- Legal and professional costs — 5.5 £
- Cost of services provided, including wages — 5.6 £
- Other expenses — 5.7 £

total of boxes 5.2 to 5.7 — 5.8 £

Net profit (put figures in brackets if a loss) — box 5.1 *less* box 5.8 — 5.9 £

■ *Tax adjustments*

- Private use — 5.10 £
- Balancing charges — 5.11 £

box 5.10 + box 5.11 — 5.12 £

- Capital allowances — 5.13 £

Profit for the period (copy to box 5.19). If loss enter '0' and put the loss in box 5.15 — boxes 5.9 + 5.12 *less* box 5.13 — 5.14 £

Loss for the period (if '0' in box 5.14) — boxes 5.9 + 5.12 *less* box 5.13 — 5.15 £

- Loss offset against 1996-97 total income — 5.16 £
- Loss carried back — see Notes, page L4 — 5.17 £
- Loss offset against other income from property (copy to box 5.38) — see Notes, page L4 — 5.18 £

Fig. 19. Property income page 1.

64

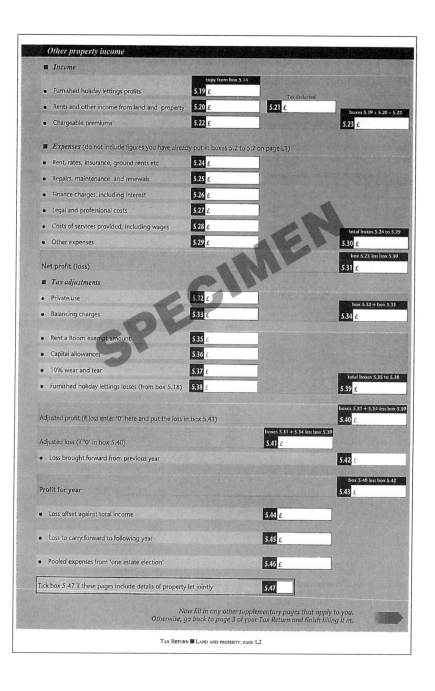

Other property income

■ *Income*

		copy from box 5.14		Tax deducted	
• Furnished holiday lettings profits	5.19 £				
• Rents and other income from land and property	5.20 £		5.21 £		
• Chargeable premiums	5.22 £				boxes 5.19 + 5.20 + 5.22
					5.23 £

■ *Expenses* (do not include figures you have already put in boxes 5.2 to 5.7 on page L1)

• Rent, rates, insurance, ground rents etc	5.24 £
• Repairs, maintenance and renewals	5.25 £
• Finance charges, including Interest	5.26 £
• Legal and professional costs	5.27 £
• Costs of services provided, including wages	5.28 £
• Other expenses	5.29 £

total boxes 5.24 to 5.29

5.30 £

Net profit (loss)

box 5.23 *less* box 5.30

5.31 £

■ *Tax adjustments*

• Private use	5.32 £
• Balancing charges	5.33 £

box 5.32 + box 5.33

5.34 £

• Rent a Room exempt amount	5.35 £
• Capital allowances	5.36 £
• 10% wear and tear	5.37 £
• Furnished holiday lettings losses (from box 5.18)	5.38 £

total boxes 5.35 to 5.38

5.39 £

Adjusted profit (if loss enter '0' here and put the loss in box 5.41)

boxes 5.31 + 5.34 *less* box 5.39

5.40 £

Adjusted loss (if '0' in box 5.40)

boxes 5.31 + 5.34 *less* box 5.39

5.41 £

• Loss brought forward from previous year

5.42 £

Profit for year

box 5.40 *less* box 5.42

5.43 £

• Loss offset against total income

5.44 £

• Loss to carry forward to following year

5.45 £

• Pooled expenses from 'one estate election'

5.46 £

Tick box 5.47 if these pages include details of property let jointly

5.47

Now fill in any other supplementary pages that apply to you.
Otherwise, go back to page 3 of your Tax Return and finish filling it in.

Fig. 20. Property income page 2.

furnished holiday lettings, shown above. These go in boxes 5.24 to 5.29. Once again, if the total income is less than £15,000, the expenses can be entered as one figure in box 5.30.

The profit or loss is shown in box 5.31.

Then make adjustments for private use, and capital allowances, as for furnished holiday lettings, in boxes 5.32 to 5.34, and box 5.36. There are two other adjustments also.

1. If your total rents included Rent a Room receipts over £3,250, claim the exempt amount of £3,250 in box 5.35.

2. If your total rents included furnished letting, then you may claim a 'wear and tear' allowance, to cover renewals of furniture. You may claim 10 per cent of the total furnished lettings rent less items which would normally be paid by the tenant, but are in fact paid by you (such as council tax). This goes in box 5.37.

Example
The tenant pays you rent of £2,000 per year, but you pay the council tax of £500. You claim wear and tear allowance of £150 (*ie* £2,000 less £500 = £1,500 x 10%).

You may choose not to claim the wear and tear allowance, but to claim the actual cost of renewals of the furniture, as and when that occurs. If you choose this method you cannot claim the original cost of the furniture – only its renewal.

Whichever method you choose, it must be applied consistently.

The profit or loss is then arrived at and put in box 5.40 for a profit or 5.41 for a loss. If there is a loss, you indicate in the final boxes how to want to use the loss, in boxes 5.44 to 5.46.

Foreign income and gains
Figure 21 shows page 1 of this section.

This page deals with foreign savings income. Enter:

- the country – column A
- tick the box if the income is unremittable
- amount before tax – column B
- UK Tax – column C
- foreign tax – column D
- amount chargeable – column E
- if you wish to claim the foreign tax credit relief, tick the box in column E.

Columns C and E are totalled.

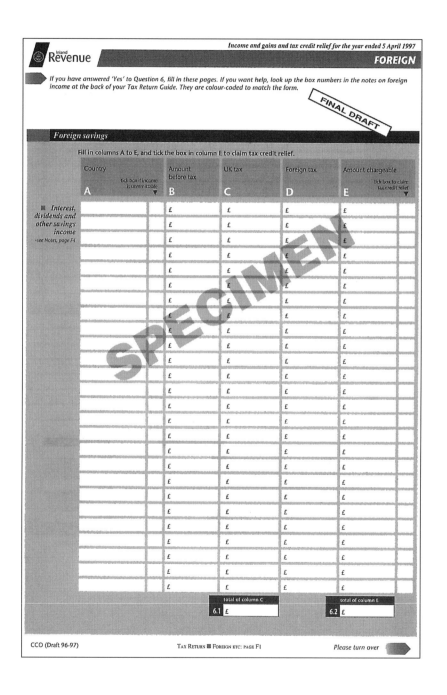

Fig.21. Foreign income page 1.

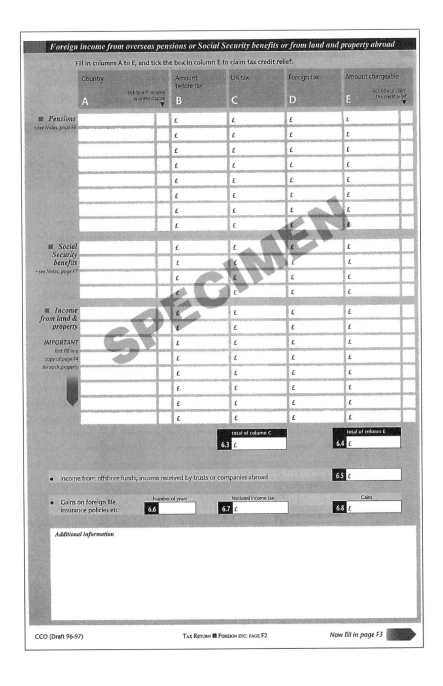

Fig. 22. Foreign income page 2.

Tax credit relief for foreign tax paid on income reported elsewhere in your Tax Return

See Notes, page F14

Enter in this column the page number in your Tax Return from which information is taken. Do this for each item for which you are claiming tax credit ▼	Country tick box if income is unremittable A		Foreign tax D	Amount chargeable tick box to claim tax credit relief E ▼
			£	£
			£	£
			£	£
			£	£
			£	£
			£	£
			£	£
			£	£
			£	£
			£	£

- If you are calculating your tax, enter the total tax credit relief on your income in box 6.9   **6.9** £

Tax credit relief for foreign tax paid on chargeable gains reported on your Capital gains pages

See Notes, page F15

Amount of gain under UK rules	Period UK gain accrued over	Amount of gain under foreign tax rules	Period foreign gain accrued over	Foreign tax paid tick box to claim tax credit relief D ▼
£	days	£	days	£
£	days	£	days	£
£	days	£	days	£
£	days	£	days	£
£	days	£	days	£
£	days	£	days	£
£	days	£	days	£
£	days	£	days	£
£	days	£	days	£

- If you are calculating your tax, enter the total tax credit relief on your gains in box 6.10   **6.10** £

Additional information

Now fill in any other supplementary pages that apply to you.
Otherwise, go back to page 3 in your Tax Return and finish filling it in.

CCO (Draft 96-97)   TAX RETURN ■ FOREIGN ETC: PAGE F3

Fig. 23. Foreign income page 3.

69

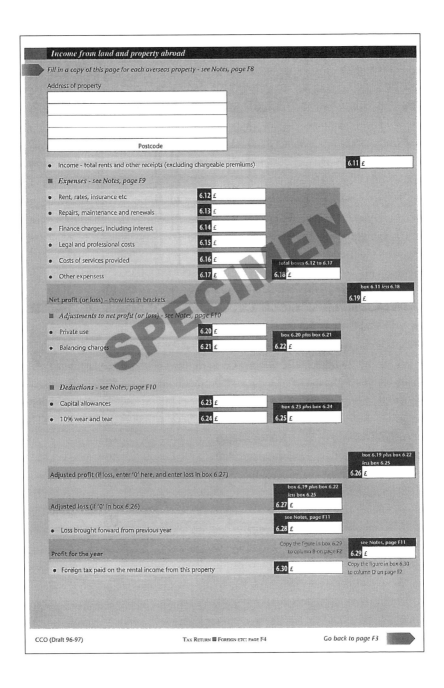

Income from land and property abroad

Fill in a copy of this page for each overseas property - see Notes, page F8

Address of property

Postcode

- Income - total rents and other receipts (excluding chargeable premiums) — 6.11 £

■ *Expenses - see Notes, page F9*

- Rent, rates, insurance etc — 6.12 £
- Repairs, maintenance and renewals — 6.13 £
- Finance charges, including interest — 6.14 £
- Legal and professional costs — 6.15 £
- Costs of services provided — 6.16 £
- Other expensess — 6.17 £ | total boxes 6.12 to 6.17 6.18 £

Net profit (or loss) – show loss in brackets | box 6.11 *less* 6.18 6.19 £

■ *Adjustments to net profit (or loss) - see Notes, page F10*

- Private use — 6.20 £
- Balancing charges — 6.21 £ | box 6.20 *plus* box 6.21 6.22 £

■ *Deductions - see Notes, page F10*

- Capital allowances — 6.23 £
- 10% wear and tear — 6.24 £ | box 6.23 *plus* box 6.24 6.25 £

Adjusted profit (if loss, enter '0' here, and enter loss in box 6.27) | box 6.19 *plus* box 6.22 *less* box 6.25 6.26 £

Adjusted loss (if '0' in box 6.26) | box 6.19 *plus* box 6.22 *less* box 6.25 6.27 £

- Loss brought forward from previous year | see Notes, page F11 6.28 £

Profit for the year | Copy the figure in box 6.29 to column B on page F2 | see Notes, page F11 6.29 £

- Foreign tax paid on the rental income from this property — 6.30 £ | Copy the figure in box 6.30 to column D on page F2.

Fig. 24. Foreign income page 4.

Figure 22 shows page 2 of this section.

Enter on this page overseas pensions or Social Security benefits, and income from land and property overseas. The columns are the same as on page 1. Again, columns C and E are totalled.

Enter income from offshore funds in box 6.5 and gains on foreign life assurance policies in boxes 6.6 to 6.8.

Figure 23 shows page 3 of this section.

In this section, claim credit for foreign tax paid on income reported elsewhere in the tax return, and on capital gains. The columns are labelled A, D and E, to correspond with the columns on the previous pages. Enter the total tax credit claimed in box 6.9 for income, and box 6.10 for capital gains.

To get the tax credit for capital gains, you must fill in the details of each gain as follows:

- gain under UK rules
- period over which the UK gain accrued
- gain under foreign rules
- period over which the foreign gain accrued.

Figure 24 shows page 4 of this section.

Enter here details of each property overseas for which income is declared on page 2. If you have more than one property, you may photocopy this page, or ask for more pages from the Inland Revenue. The details in boxes 6.11 to 6.29 are the same as the boxes in the section for property income in this country, and box 6.30 is for foreign tax paid on property income.

There are some points which need to be kept in mind regarding foreign income:

- Normally, your overseas income is taxed in the period when it arises, not the time it is brought into this country. For example, if you received interest on a foreign investment on 31 March, but did not bring it into this country until 30 April, it has to be reported in this country in the first tax year ending on 5 April.

- However, if you claim to be:
  - resident in the UK, but not permanently domiciled here
  - resident in the UK and a citizen of the Republic of Ireland or the Commonwealth, and not ordinarily resident in the UK
  then you are only taxed on the income you actually bring into the UK. This is known as the 'remittance basis'. There are two exceptions to this, however:
  1. Gains under a life assurance policy.

2. Income from Republic of Ireland pensions, securities, stocks, shares and rents.

Income under these exceptions is taxed under the normal 'arising' basis.

Residence, Ordinary Residence, and Domicile can be fairly complicated matters, and they are dealt with under the final section of supplementary sheets.

- **Unremittable income**: if you have foreign income which you cannot send to this country (for example due to foreign exchange restrictions) then it is not taxable in the UK. It has to be shown on these sheets, but you tick the box showing that it is unremittable.

- **Rate of exchange**: on the normal 'arising' basis, calculate the exchange on the date the income arose. On the 'remittance' basis, calculate the exchange on the date the money was remitted to this country. If you do not know these rates, your local tax office can help you.

The details to be shown are the country involved, an indication of whether the amount was unremittable (by ticking a box), the gross amount, the UK tax suffered, the foreign tax suffered, and the amount chargeable.

Normally the amount chargeable will be the same as the gross amount. However, for unremittable income and remittance basis, this may not be so.

Unremittable income is shown in the currency of the country (by crossing through the £ sign), and nothing is shown in the 'amount chargeable' column.

For the remittance basis, the amount to be shown is the proportion actually sent to this country.

Example
You earned £1,000, and suffered £200 foreign tax. Out of the £800 remaining, you sent £400 to this country. You then enter £500 as chargeable, with £100 as foreign tax suffered.

Warning
Some dividends from UK countries show 'Foreign Income Dividends'. These should not be shown in this section. They represent a special treatment for the UK dividends received, and are shown on page 3 of your tax return.

Income from trusts and estates of deceased persons

Figure 25 shows page 1 of this section.

If you received income from a trust or from a deceased person's estate, enter the amounts in this section. Do *not* enter any legacies from deceased persons, or any residue of the estate. However, if you receive from the executor a statement of the amount of any residue, it may include a part described as income. That part should be noted on the 'Additional information' part of this section.

Otherwise, any amounts you receive from trusts or estates should be certified by a form R185 which the trustee or executor should send you. The R185 will show the gross income, which parts are taxed at the basic rate of 24 per cent and which parts are taxed at the lower rate of 20 per cent. Enter these amounts in the boxes provided.

Income from trusts is shown in boxes 7.1 to 7.6.

Income from estates of deceased persons is shown in boxes 7.7 to 7.19.

The income from estates may show non-repayable income at either the basic rate or the lower rate. If so, show this in boxes 7.14 to 7.18.

Capital gains

Figure 26 shows page 1 of this section.

Capital gains (or losses) are made on the disposal of assets. It can also apply in certain circumstances to sums derived from an asset, even when there was no disposal.

Page 1 is for the calculation of the taxable amount. Show the detailed figures on page 2. The gain brought forward goes into box 8.1.

Deduct losses for the same year in box 8.2

This leaves either a net gain (in box 8.3) or a net loss (in box 8.4).

If you want to claim business losses against the capital gain, enter the amount in box 8.5. Enter losses brought forward from previous years in box 8.6.

This leaves a final amount (called the 'chargeable gain') in box 8.7.

Deduct the threshold amount (£6,300 for 1996/97) to arrive at the taxable amount in box 8.8. If there is additional liability for offshore trusts, it goes in box 8.9. Help sheet IR 301 tells you how to calculate this.

The bottom half is for you to keep a record of your losses:

1. Enter unused losses brought forward in box 8.10.
2. Enter any losses you used in the year in box 8.11.

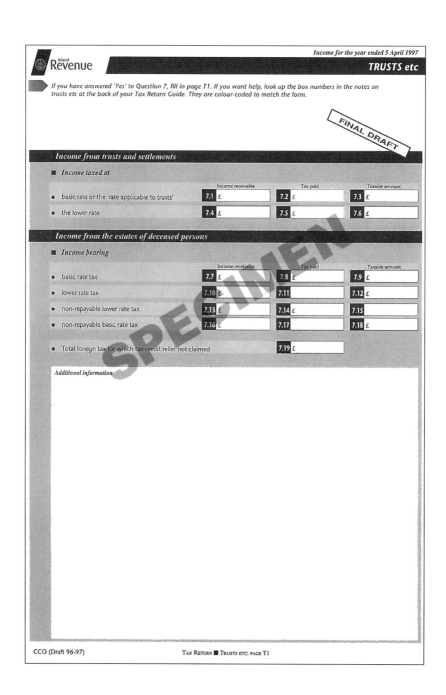

Inland Revenue

TRUSTS etc

If you have answered 'Yes' to Question 7, fill in page T1. If you want help, look up the box numbers in the notes on trusts etc at the back of your Tax Return Guide. They are colour-coded to match the form.

FINAL DRAFT

Income from trusts and settlements

■ **Income taxed at**

	Income receivable	Tax paid	Taxable amount
● basic rate or the 'rate applicable to trusts'	**7.1** £	**7.2** £	**7.3** £
● the lower rate	**7.4** £	**7.5** £	**7.6** £

Income from the estates of deceased persons

■ **Income bearing**

	Income receivable	Tax paid	Taxable amount
● basic rate tax	**7.7** £	**7.8** £	**7.9** £
● lower rate tax	**7.10** £	**7.11**	**7.12** £
● non-repayable lower rate tax	**7.13** £	**7.14** £	**7.15**
● non-repayable basic rate tax	**7.16** £	**7.17**	**7.18** £
● Total foreign tax for which tax credit relief not claimed		**7.19** £	

Additional information

Fig. 25. Trust income page 1.

74

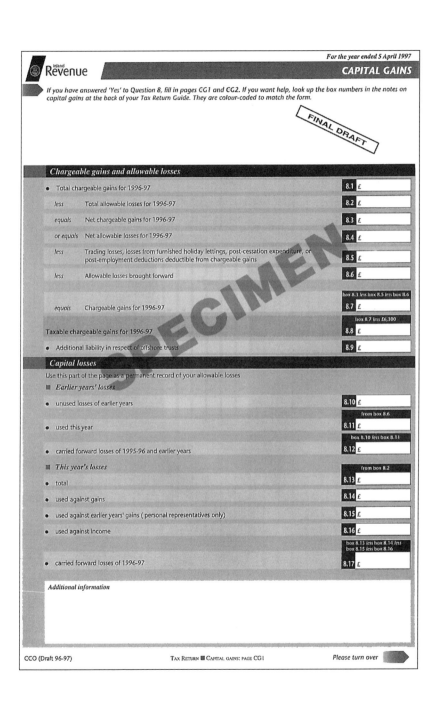

Revenue Inland

CAPITAL GAINS

If you have answered 'Yes' to Question 8, fill in pages CG1 and CG2. If you want help, look up the box numbers in the notes on capital gains at the back of your Tax Return Guide. They are colour-coded to match the form.

FINAL DRAFT

Chargeable gains and allowable losses

- Total chargeable gains for 1996-97 — **8.1** £

less Total allowable losses for 1996-97 — **8.2** £

equals Net chargeable gains for 1996-97 — **8.3** £

or equals Net allowable losses for 1996-97 — **8.4** £

less Trading losses, losses from furnished holiday lettings, post-cessation expenditure, or post-employment deductions deductible from chargeable gains — **8.5** £

less Allowable losses brought forward — **8.6** £

equals Chargeable gains for 1996-97 — box 8.3 *less* box 8.5 *less* box 8.6 **8.7** £

Taxable chargeable gains for 1996-97 — box 8.7 *less* £6,300 **8.8** £

- Additional liability in respect of offshore trusts — **8.9** £

Capital losses

Use this part of the page as a permanent record of your allowable losses

■ Earlier years' losses

- unused losses of earlier years — **8.10** £

- used this year — from box 8.6 **8.11** £

- carried forward losses of 1995-96 and earlier years — box 8.10 *less* box 8.11 **8.12** £

■ This year's losses

- total — from box 8.2 **8.13** £

- used against gains — **8.14** £

- used against earlier years' gains (personal representatives only) — **8.15** £

- used against income — **8.16** £

- carried forward losses of 1996-97 — box 8.13 *less* box 8.14 *less* box 8.15 *less* box 8.16 **8.17** £

Additional information

CCO (Draft 96-97)   TAX RETURN ■ CAPITAL GAINS: PAGE CG1   *Please turn over*

Fig. 26. Capital gains page 1.

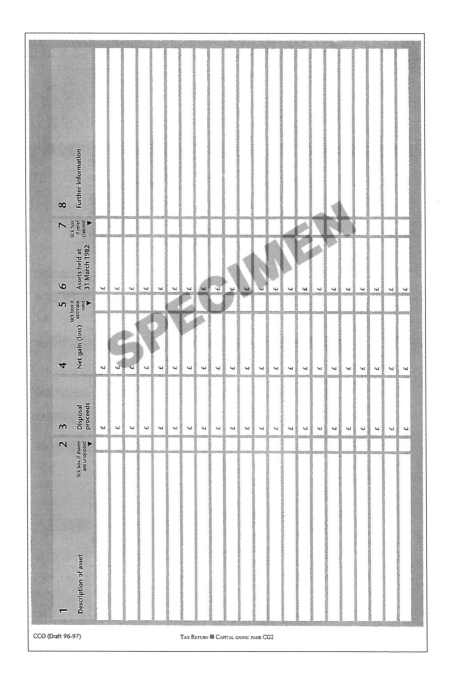

Fig. 27. Capital gains page 2.

76

3. That leaves losses from previous years carried forward in box 8.12.

4. Enter losses for the current year in box 8.13, and the amount used against current gains in box 8.14.

5. If any losses have been carried back, enter in box 8.15. (This is only allowed for personal representatives of deceased persons.)

6. If any losses have been used against income, enter in box 8.16. That then leaves the amount of current year losses to carry forward.

Thus, you may have losses carried forward to future years from both this year and from previous years.

Figure 27 shows page 2 of this section.

The gain is calculated by taking the amount you received from the asset, then deducting:

• cost incurred in disposing of the asset (*eg* fees for selling a property)
• the original cost of buying or acquiring the asset
• indexation allowance on the cost of the asset.

Cost of asset

The original cost of acquiring the asset is usually quite simple. If you bought some shares, say, and are selling them, it is simply the cost of buying those shares. However, there are some cases where it is not straightforward.

1. If you inherit an asset from a deceased person, use the probate value as your cost of acquisition.

2. If you held assets at 31 March 1982, you may have made an election for all those assets to be rebased at their market value at that date. This is usually advantageous. The market value at that date is then used as your acquisition value.

3. If you bought an asset from a 'connected person' such as a close relative, use the market value as your acquisition cost.

4. If you acquired an asset, then improved or extended it (such as a house or other property), you may add the costs of improvement to the acquisition costs.

5. If you have a 'wasting asset' (one which has a predicted life of less than 50 years), its cost is written off over its predicted life.

Thus, the amount you are allowed to deduct is not the full amount you paid for it. The write off is not done in a 'straight line', but is done according to tables supplied by the Inland Revenue in help sheet IR 293.

Indexation
Indexation allowance is a special allowance given to account for inflation. It is based on the Retail Price Index published every month. You are given as an allowance the percentage increase between the date you acquired the asset (or 31 March 1982 if later) and the date you sold it.

Example
You sell an asset on 31 March 1997 for £15,000. You bought it on 1 March 1990 for £10,000. The increase in the Retail Price Index between those dates is, say, 30 per cent. Your calculation is:

	£	£
Sale price		15,000
Cost	10,000	
Indexation	3,000	
		13,000
Gain		2,000

Exemptions
Certain assets are exempt from capital gains tax. They are listed on page CG4 of the notes. You may disregard any gains under these headings.

Private residences
In the list on page CG4, there is an exemption for your private residence. However, there are some points to consider here. If you have more than one house, you must make an election for capital gains tax purposes for one of them to be considered as your main residence. The other house is not exempt from capital gains tax.

If you have a house which has not been your private residence for part of the time that you owned it, that part is not exempt. This is done by taking a proportion of the total time you owned the house, and dividing the gain in that proportion.

Example

You owned a house from 1 January 1987 to 31 December 1996 – exactly ten years. When you sold it you made a gain of £50,000. For the first two years that you owned it, you let it out, then you moved into it and it was your private residence. The gain is divided between the first two years and the last eight years. Therefore, £10,000 is chargeable to capital gains tax, and £40,000 is exempt.

Losses

If the calculations show a loss, it is first used in offsetting other gains of the same year, then carried forward against future gains.

Warning:

A loss cannot be created or increased by indexation. Indexation can only reduce a gain.

Examples

1. You sold an asset for £10,000 on 31 March 1997. You bought it on 1 January 1990 for £12,000. There is a loss of £2,000. You may not increase this loss by indexation.

2. You sold an asset on 31 March 1997 for £11,000. You bought it on 1 January 1990 for £10,000. The indexation allowance is 30 per cent. The total indexation figure is therefore £3,000. This would have made the total to deduct from the sale price £13,000, giving a loss of £2,000. However, a loss cannot be created by indexation, so the asset is treated as sold with no gain and no loss. All the indexation does is to reduce the gain to nil.

Losses made in the same year as gains are deducted from the amount of the gains. For example:

3. You sell several assets in the tax year. Some of them make gains, which total £10,000. Others make losses of £5,000. These are all counted together in the same tax year to give a net gain of £5,000.

4. You sell several assets in the tax year. Some make gains of £5,000. Others make losses of £10,000. These are all counted together in the tax year to give a loss of £5,000. You can use this figure against future gains.

Losses may be carried forward to offset future gains. From 1997/98 onwards, you may use only enough of the losses as you need to reduce your gains to the threshold amount. For example:

5. Your losses carried forward from 1996/97 were £6,000. You make gains in 1997/98 of £10,000. The threshold allowance for 1997/98 is, say, £6,500. The calculation is:

	£	£
Gains 1997/98		10,000
Losses brought forward from 1996/97	6,000	
Losses used for 1997/98		3,500
Losses not used and available to carry forward again	2,500	
Net gain for 1997/98		6,500
(no tax due)		

The amount against which you may set losses brought forward is the net amount of your losses in a tax year. In other words, losses of the same tax year have to be set off against gains before any losses brought forward can be used.

Time limit
The losses must be claimed within **five years** of the date for filing the tax return of the tax year in which they were made. The latest date for claiming losses for the year ended 5 April 1997 is 31 January 2003. However, once claimed, a loss may be carried forward indefinitely against future gains.

Non-residence
Figure 28 shows page 1 of this section.
    This section deals with your residence status. This can be under several categories. You can be:

1. Resident or not resident in the UK.
2. Ordinarily resident or not ordinarily resident in the UK.
3. Domiciled or non-domiciled in the UK.

Resident status depends on the number of days you were in the UK during the tax year. The questions in the notes help you decide whether you were resident.
    Ordinarily resident status denotes a more permanent residence, and questions in the notes ask about your movements and intentions over the past four years. This helps you decide whether you were ordinarily resident.
    Domicile is a different concept. It indicates your permanent home. You acquire a domicile of origin from your father when you are born. After the age of 16, you may acquire a domicile of choice by

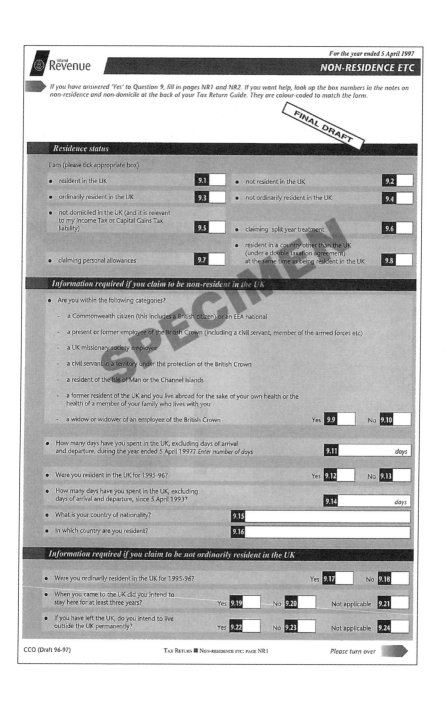

Fig. 28. Non-residence page 1.

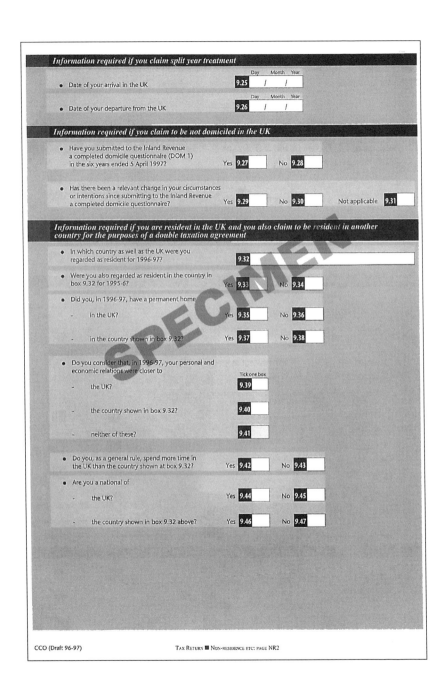

Information required if you claim split year treatment

- Date of your arrival in the UK — 9.25 [Day / Month / Year]

- Date of your departure from the UK — 9.26 [Day / Month / Year]

Information required if you claim to be not domiciled in the UK

- Have you submitted to the Inland Revenue a completed domicile questionnaire (DOM 1) in the six years ended 5 April 1997? — Yes 9.27 No 9.28

- Has there been a relevant change in your circumstances or intentions since submitting to the Inland Revenue a completed domicile questionnaire? — Yes 9.29 No 9.30 Not applicable 9.31

Information required if you are resident in the UK and you also claim to be resident in another country for the purposes of a double taxation agreement

- In which country as well as the UK were you regarded as resident for 1996-97? — 9.32

- Were you also regarded as resident in the country in box 9.32 for 1995-6? — Yes 9.33 No 9.34

- Did you, in 1996-97, have a permanent home
  - in the UK? — Yes 9.35 No 9.36
  - in the country shown in box 9.32? — Yes 9.37 No 9.38

- Do you consider that, in 1996-97, your personal and economic relations were closer to [Tick one box]
  - the UK? — 9.39
  - the country shown in box 9.32? — 9.40
  - neither of these? — 9.41

- Do you, as a general rule, spend more time in the UK than the country shown at box 9.32? — Yes 9.42 No 9.43

- Are you a national of
  - the UK? — Yes 9.44 No 9.45
  - the country shown in box 9.32 above? — Yes 9.46 No 9.47

Fig. 29. Non-residence page 2.

82

settling in another country. You may also acquire a domicile of dependency by marriage.

You may, therefore, answer positive to one category, but negative to another. For instance, you may be resident but not ordinarily resident in the UK. You may be domiciled in the UK but not resident during the tax year.

Claiming 'split year' treatment

You may also claim 'split year' treatment. Normally, you can only be considered either resident or non-resident in the UK for any tax year. However, when you leave the UK permanently, or arrive in the UK permanently, you may claim the 'split year' treatment. This is a concessionary treatment allowed by the Inland Revenue. Broadly, it means that your income is considered as liable to UK tax only for the period you are in the UK. Decide whether you may claim by going through the questions on the notes pages.

Tick the boxes on page 1 to declare whether you were or were not resident, ordinarily resident, domiciled, or claiming the split year treatment in the UK during the tax year. These determine the way in which your tax liability is calculated.

If you claim to be non-resident, answer the questions in boxes 9.9 to 9.16.

If you claim to be not ordinarily resident, answer the questions in boxes 9.17 to 9.24.

Figure 29 shows page 2 of this section.

If you claim split year treatment, answer the questions in boxes 9.25 and 9.26, about the dates of your arrival and/or departure in the UK.

If you claim to be not domiciled in the UK answer the questions in boxes 9.27 to 9.31.

If you are resident in the UK and another country, answer the questions in boxes 9.32 to 9.47.

This finishes the supplementary pages. Now go back to the main tax return for step 3.

Step 3

This step involves answering the rest of the questions on the remaining six pages of the tax return form. Each question starts with a 'yes' or 'no' answer. If the answer is 'yes', fill in the details which follow. If the answer is 'no', go on to the next question.

Savings and investment income

Figure 30 shows page 3 of the tax return.

If you received any savings or investment income, declare it on this page. The income is divided between interest and dividends.

Interest
Interest is declared in the boxes under various headings. If you had more than one item under any heading, prepare a list showing the different items making up the total. The headings are:

		Box
1.	Bank and building society interest without tax deducted	10.1
2.	Bank and building society interest with tax deducted	10.2 to 10.4
3.	Interest from unit trusts	10.5 to 10.7
4.	Interest from National Savings (except FIRST Option Bonds)	10.8
5.	Interest from National Savings FIRST Option Bonds	10.9 to 10.11
6.	Any other interest	10.12 to 10.14

Dividends
Dividends are different from interest. **Interest** is a payment made to you on a loan or account of some sort. It is paid to you according to the rates of interest attaching to the loan or account. **Dividends** are a return on shares (or units in a unit trust) which represent a participation in the profits of the company or unit trust. The rate of dividend you receive depends on the amount of profit made, in the case of ordinary shares, or at a fixed rate in the case of preference shares.

Tip: If you are in any doubt about whether the amount you receive is interest or dividend, look at the certificate. If it shows a gross amount and tax deducted, it is interest. If it shows a net amount and a tax credit, it is a dividend.

Dividends are shown under several different headings:

		Box
1.	Dividends from UK companies	10.15 to 10.17
2.	Dividends from UK unit trusts	10.18 to 10.20
3.	Scrip dividends from UK companies	10.21 to 10.23
4.	Foreign income dividends from UK companies	10.24 to 10.26

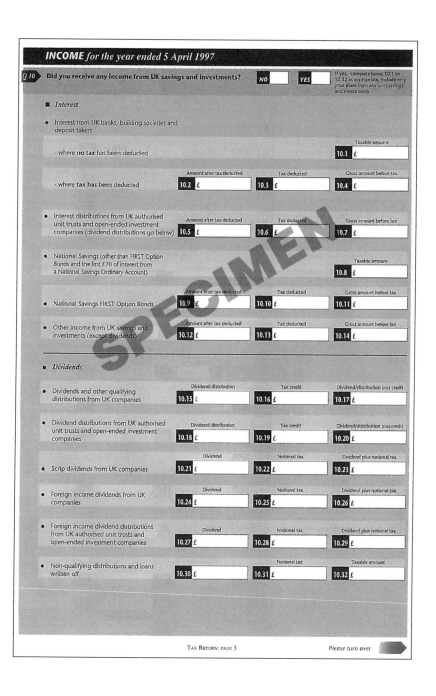

Fig. 30. Tax return page 3.

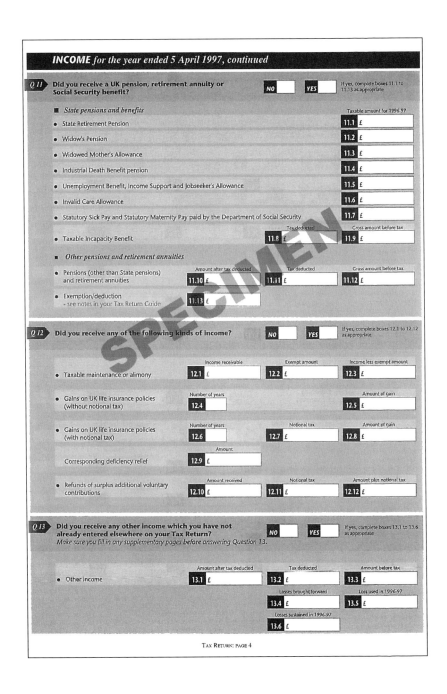

INCOME *for the year ended 5 April 1997, continued*

Q 11 Did you receive a UK pension, retirement annuity or Social Security benefit?   NO [ ]   YES [ ]   If yes, complete boxes 11.1 to 11.13 as appropriate

■ *State pensions and benefits*   Taxable amount for 1996-97

- State Retirement Pension   11.1 £
- Widow's Pension   11.2 £
- Widowed Mother's Allowance   11.3 £
- Industrial Death Benefit pension   11.4 £
- Unemployment Benefit, Income Support and Jobseeker's Allowance   11.5 £
- Invalid Care Allowance   11.6 £
- Statutory Sick Pay and Statutory Maternity Pay paid by the Department of Social Security   11.7 £

	Tax deducted	Gross amount before tax
• Taxable Incapacity Benefit	11.8 £	11.9 £

■ *Other pensions and retirement annuities*

	Amount after tax deducted	Tax deducted	Gross amount before tax
• Pensions (other than State pensions) and retirement annuities	11.10 £	11.11 £	11.12 £
• Exemption/deduction - see notes in your Tax Return Guide	11.13 £		

Q 12 Did you receive any of the following kinds of income?   NO [ ]   YES [ ]   If yes, complete boxes 12.1 to 12.12 as appropriate

	Income receivable	Exempt amount	Income less exempt amount
• Taxable maintenance or alimony	12.1 £	12.2 £	12.3 £

	Number of years		Amount of gain
• Gains on UK life insurance policies (without notional tax)	12.4		12.5 £

	Number of years	Notional tax	Amount of gain
• Gains on UK life insurance policies (with notional tax)	12.6	12.7 £	12.8 £

	Amount		
Corresponding deficiency relief	12.9 £		

	Amount received	Notional tax	Amount plus notional tax
• Refunds of surplus additional voluntary contributions	12.10 £	12.11 £	12.12 £

Q 13 Did you receive any other income which you have not already entered elsewhere on your Tax Return?   NO [ ]   YES [ ]   If yes, complete boxes 13.1 to 13.6 as appropriate
Make sure you fill in any supplementary pages before answering Question 13.

	Amount after tax deducted	Tax deducted	Amount before tax
• Other income	13.1 £	13.2 £	13.3 £

	Losses brought forward	Loss used in 1996-97
	13.4 £	13.5 £

	Losses sustained in 1996-97
	13.6 £

TAX RETURN: PAGE 4

Fig. 31 Tax return page 4.

5. Foreign income dividends from UK unit trusts 10.27 to 10.29
6. Non-qualifying distributions and loans written
   off   10.30 to 10.33

Scrip dividends
Scrip dividends are dividends which you receive in the form of extra shares rather than in cash. The tax credit on them is not repayable to you, but it is counted as part of the tax you have already suffered.

Foreign income dividends
These are dividends from a company or unit trust which has part of its income deriving from foreign countries. If they declare part or all of their dividends under the foreign income dividend scheme, the dividend voucher will show this clearly. The foreign income dividends must be shown separately. The tax credit on foreign income dividends is not repayable to you, but counts as part of the tax you have already suffered.

Non-qualifying distributions or loans written off
These are rare. If a company gives a bonus issue of redeemable shares, it is considered as a non-qualifying distribution, and carries a tax credit.

If you are a shareholder in a company, and have also made a loan to the company, then the company writes off that loan, it is considered as a non-qualifying distribution, carrying a tax credit.

UK pensions, retirement annuities or Social Security benefits
Figure 31 shows page 4 of the tax return.

This section is to declare income under the following categories:

		Box
1.	State retirement pension	11.1
2.	Widow's pension	11.2
3.	Widowed mother's allowance	11.3
4.	Industrial death benefit pension	11.4
5.	Unemployment benefit, income support and jobseeker's allowance	11.5
6.	Invalid care allowance	11.6
7.	Statutory sick pay and statutory maternity pay (when paid by the DSS)	11.7
8.	Taxable incapacity benefit	11.8 to 11.9
9.	Other pensions and retirement annuities	11.10 to 11.13

Under each heading there are things to include or exclude:

Heading	Include	Exclude
State retirement pension	Basic pension SERPS addition Graduated pension Age addition for over 80s Incapacity addition Dependent adult addition Increases to uprate a guaranteed minimum	Christmas bonus
Widow's pension	Full amount	
Widowed mother's allowance	Flat rate basic allowance	Child dependency increase
Industrial death benefit pension	Annual amount under industrial death benefit scheme	Industrial death benefit child allowance
Unemployment benefit, income support and jobseeker's allowance	The amount shown as taxable on the statement given to you	
Invalid care allowance	The basic entitlement including dependent adult addition	Dependent child addition
Statutory sick pay and statutory maternity pay when paid by the DSS	Total received in the year	
Incapacity benefit	The amount shown as taxable on the form given to you	Benefit paid for the first 26 weeks Benefit which began before 13 April 1995
Other pensions and retirement annuities	The amount shown on P60 (and tax deducted)	

Exemptions or deductions
Some pensions are exempt from tax or are eligible for a 10 per cent deduction. These are:

- If you get a pension because you are retired due to an industrial injury, or an industrial illness, and the pension you get is more than the normal amount for someone retiring at your age, on ordinary ill health grounds, the extra amount is **exempt** from tax.

- If you get a pension for war injuries, or wounds or disability in military service, it is **exempt** from tax.

- If you receive an official pension from the UK government or foreign government for service in Commonwealth countries (or territories under Her Majesty's protection), it is subject to a **10 per cent deduction**.

Other income
The next two sections deal with the final pieces of information for other income. They are:

		Box
1.	Taxable maintenance or alimony	12.1 to 12.3
2.	Gains on UK life assurance policies	12.4 to 12.9
3.	Refunds of surplus additional voluntary contributions	12.10 to 12.12
4.	Any other income not declared elsewhere	13.1 to 13.6

Taxable maintenance or alimony
You are liable to tax on these amounts received by you if they are made under:

- a court order made before 15 March 1988

- a written agreement made before 15 March 1988 (if that agreement was received by the Inspector of Taxes before 30 June 1988)

- a verbal agreement made before 15 March 1988 (if the details were given in writing to the Inspector of Taxes before 30 June 1988)

- a court order, CSA assessment or written agreement made after 15 March 1988 which varies any such order dated before 15 March 1988.

The amount you are taxed on is the lower of the amount you received in the 1996/97 tax year and the amount you received in the 1988/89 tax year.

You may also claim the exempt amount (£1,790) if all of the following apply:

- the payments are from your separated or former husband or wife
- they are for you or children under age 21
- you have not remarried
- you did not live again with your separated or ex-husband or wife.

Gains on life assurance policies
The only amounts taxable are on 'non-qualifying' policies (*ie* which do not meet the following tests):

- The policy must have had a minimum term of ten years, or be a whole of life policy (in other words one that paid out on death only).
- Regular premiums must have been paid in each of the ten or more years of the policy.

In practice, non-qualifying policies are usually single premium policies, often called **bonds**. If you have surrendered such a policy, or it has matured, the insurance company will issue you with a 'chargeable event certificate'. The gain on this chargeable event is only taxable if you are a higher rate tax payer, or if your total income would restrict your age allowance.

Refunds of surplus additional voluntary contributions
If you left a job or retired, you may have had a refund of additional voluntary contributions to a pension fund. When this happens, the pension scheme deducts tax, and pays you the net amount. They will give you a certificate showing the gross amount, tax deducted, and the net amount. Enter that here.

Any other income
If there is any other form of income that is not declared anywhere else, it is entered here on the last part of the tax return to deal with income. The tax return notes give examples.

The list is not exhaustive. If you have any other sort of income, it must be declared here. There may also have been losses under any of these headings which might otherwise have made a profit, and these losses are claimed here.

Reliefs

Figure 32 shows page 5 of the tax return.

This page is for claiming reliefs. Reliefs are amounts given against your tax liability for certain types of payment you have made.

Pensions

Pension contributions can come under different headings.

Retirement annuities

These were a type of policy that finished in 1988. However, there are many people with these type of policies still running, and relief is still available. They were only available to self employed people.

Personal pension plans

These policies replaced retirement annuities, and were available to self employed people and employed people. Some of the conditions are different from the old retirement annuities (such as the age at which you may take the benefits).

While you are paying premiums into the policies, you may claim tax relief on them, whether your policy is an old retirement annuity or a new personal pension. There are limits on the amount for which you can claim tax relief, and these differ slightly between the two types of policy. The limits are related to your 'net relevant earnings'. This means income from the following:

- earnings from a non-pensionable employment
- self employed profits as a sole trader
- self employed profits as a partner
- profits from furnished holiday letting.

The limit also varies according to your age at the *beginning* of the tax year. The limits are shown in the following table as a percentage of net relevant earnings.

Age at beginning of tax year	Personal pension limit (%)	Retirement annuity limit (%)
Up to 35	17.5	17.5
36 to 45	20	17.5
46 to 50	25	17.5
51 to 55	30	20
56 to 60	35	22.5
61 to 74	40	27.5

RELIEFS *for the year ended 5 April 1997*

Q 14 **Do you want to claim relief for pension contributions?** | NO | YES | If yes, fill in boxes 14.1 to 14.17 below as appropriate

Do not include contributions deducted from your pay by your employer because tax relief is given automatically.

■ *Retirement annuity contracts*

| Payments made in 1996-97 | **14.1** £ | 1996-97 payments used in an earlier year | **14.2** £ | **Relief claimed** box 14.1 *less* box 14.2 *less* box 14.3 |
| 1996-97 payments now to be carried back | **14.3** £ | Payments brought back from 1997-98 | **14.4** £ | **14.5** £ |

■ *Self-employed contributions to personal pension plans*

| Payments made in 1996-97 | **14.6** £ | 1996-97 payments used in an earlier year | **14.7** £ | **Relief claimed** box 14.6 *less* box 14.7 *less* box 14.8 |
| 1996-97 payments now to be carried back | **14.8** £ | Payments brought back from 1997-98 | **14.9** £ | **14.10** £ |

■ *Employee contributions to personal pension plans* (remember to include basic rate tax by dividing your payment by 76 and then multiplying by 100 - see note on box 14.11 in your Tax Return Guide)

| Payments made in 1996-97 | **14.11** £ | 1996-97 payments used in an earlier year | **14.12** £ | **Relief claimed** box 14.11 *less* box 14.12 *less* box 14.13 |
| 1996-97 payments now to be carried back | **14.13** £ | Payments brought back from 1997-98 | **14.14** £ | **14.15** £ |

- Amount of contributions to employer's schemes **not deducted** at source from pay — **14.16** £
- Gross amount of free-standing additional voluntary contributions paid in 1996-97 — **14.17** £

Q 15 **Do you want to claim any of the following reliefs?** | NO | YES | If yes, fill in boxes 15.1 to 15.12 below, as appropriate

- Payments you made for vocational training | Amount of payment **15.1** £
- Interest on loans to purchase your main home (other than MIRAS) | **15.2** £
- Interest on other qualifying loans | **15.3** £
- Maintenance or alimony payments you have made under a court order, Child Support Agency assessment or legally binding order or agreement | Amount claimed under 'new' rules **15.4** £
  - Amount claimed under 'old' rules up to £1,790 **15.5** £ | Amount claimed under 'old' rules over £1,790 **15.6** £
- Subscriptions for Venture Capital Trust shares (up to £100,000) | Amount on which relief claimed **15.7** £
- Subscriptions under the Enterprise Investment Scheme (up to £100,000) | **15.8** £
- Charitable covenants or annuities | Amount of payment **15.9** £
- Gift Aid | Amount of payment **15.10** £
- Post-cessation expenses, and losses on relevant discounted securities | Amount of payment **15.11** £
- Payments to a trade union or friendly society for death benefits | Half amount of payment **15.12** £

TAX RETURN: PAGE 5

Please turn over ▶

Fig. 32. Tax return page 5.

If you make contributions to both types of policies, apply the percentage limit for retirement annuities first, then use up any extra percentage allowance on personal pensions, but you must take into account any retirement annuities you have paid.

Example

You are age 40, self employed, and your profit figure assessed for 1996/97 is £20,000. You pay premiums to a retirement annuity policy of £3,000, and to a personal pension policy of £1,500.

Your relief for retirement annuities is a maximum of 17.5% of £20,000 – *ie* £3,500. The premiums you paid are less than that, so they are all allowed. Your relief for personal pensions is 20% of £20,000 – *ie* £4,000, less the amount you have already claimed under retirement annuity. Therefore, your maximum relief is £4,000 counting both retirement annuities and personal pensions. You have paid a total of £4,500, so you have £500 which cannot be relieved against tax unless one of the other provisions allows it.

Carrying back and carrying forward

You may elect to **carry back** a premium paid to the previous year. This means that if you make the election, the relief you get is calculated as if the payment had been made in the previous year. This has to be done within the right time limit – 31 January following the tax year in which you paid the premiums. This might be advantageous where, for example, you paid a higher tax rate in the previous tax year.

You may also **carry forward** unused relief for up to six years. This means that if the maximum relief available has not been used in a year, the surplus may be carried forward up to six years ahead. This allows premiums paid in excess of the allowance to be used for tax purposes. Thus, in the example above, the excess £500 paid could be allowed against tax if there were unused allowances brought forward from an earlier year. The full allowance for the current year must, of course, be used up before any relief brought forward is available.

Example

In 1995/96, your self employed profits were £30,000. You were aged 40. You paid premiums to a personal pension policy of £3,000. Your percentage allowance was 20 per cent, so your maximum allowance was £6,000. You only used £3,000 for relief, so there is £3,000 available to carry forward up to six years.

If your self employed profits in 1996/97 were £10,000, and you paid the same premium, £3,000, then your allowance amount is

ALLOWANCES *for the year ended 5 April 1997*

Q 16 You get your personal allowance of £3,765 automatically. If you were born before 6 April 1932, enter your date of birth in box 21.4 to get age-related allowances. Fill in other boxes as appropriate.

Do you want to claim any of the following allowances?   NO [ ]   YES [ ]   *If yes, fill in boxes 16.1 to 16.28 as appropriate*

■ *Blind person's allowance*   Date of registration (if first year of claim) **16.1** [/ /]   Local authority (or other register) **16.2** [ ]

■ *Transitional allowance* (for some wives with husbands on low income if claimed in earlier years)

- Tick to claim and give details in the 'Additional information' box on page 8 please
  (see page 23 of your Tax Return Guide for what is needed)   **16.3** [ ]

- If you want to calculate your tax enter amount of transitional allowance you can have in box 16.4   **16.4** £ [ ]

■ *Married couple's allowance - if you are a married man* - *see page 24 of your Tax Return Guide*

- Wife's full name   **16.5** [ ]

- Date of marriage (if after 5 April 1996)   **16.6** [/ /]

- Wife's date of birth (if before 6 April 1932)   **16.7** [/ /]

- Tick box 16.8 if you and your wife have allocated half the allowance to her   **16.8** [ ]

- Wife's tax reference (if known, please)   **16.9** [ ]

- Tick box 16.10 if you and your wife have allocated all the allowance to her   **16.10** [ ]

■ *Married couple's allowance - if you are a married woman* - *see page 23 of your Tax Return Guide*

- Date of marriage (if after 5 April 1996)   **16.11** [/ /]

- Husband's full name   **16.12** [ ]

- Tick box 16.13 if you and your husband have allocated half the allowance to you   **16.13** [ ]

- Husband's tax reference (if known, please)   **16.14** [ ]

- Tick box 16.15 if you and your husband have allocated all the allowance to you   **16.15** [ ]

■ *Additional personal allowance* (available in some circumstances if you have a child living with you - *see page 24 of your Tax Return Guide*)

- Name of the child claimed for   **16.16** [ ]

- Child's date of birth   **16.17** [/ /]

- Tick if child lives with you   **16.18** [ ]

- Name of university etc/type of training if child 16 or over on 6 April 1996 and in full time education or training   **16.19** [ ]

Shared claims
Name and address of other person claiming
16.20 [ ]

Postcode

- Enter your share as a percentage   **16.21** [ ] %

- If share not agreed, enter number of days in year ended 5 April 1997 child lived with
  - you   **16.22** [ ] days
  - other person   **16.23** [ ] days

■ *Widow's bereavement allowance*   • Date of your husband's death   **16.24** [/ /]

■ *Transfer of surplus allowances* - *see page 25 of your Tax Return Guide before you fill in boxes 16.25 to 16.28*

- Tick if you want your spouse to have your unused allowances   **16.25** [ ]

- Tick if you want to have your spouse's unused allowances   **16.26** [ ]

Please give details in the 'Additional information' box on page 8 (see page 25 of your Tax Return Guide to see what is needed)
If you want to calculate your tax enter the amount of the surplus allowance you can have.

- Blind person's surplus allowance   **16.27** £ [ ]

- Married couple's surplus allowance   **16.28** £ [ ]

TAX RETURN: PAGE 6

Fig.33. Tax return page 6.

£2,000 only (20 per cent of £10,000). You had paid excess premiums of £1,000. However, you have £3,000 of allowances brought forward from the previous year to use up. Therefore, you have used up £1,000 of those allowances, and the full £3,000 is relievable against tax. You then have £2,000 left of the allowance from 1995/96 to carry forward again to use until the 2001/2002 tax year.

Enter your claims for relief for pension payments and carry backs or carry forwards in boxes 14.1 to 14.17.

Other reliefs
The bottom half of the page is for claiming other reliefs as follows:

	Box
1. Vocational training	15.1
2. Home purchase loan interest (unless it is on MIRAS)	15.2
3. Interest on other qualifying loans	15.3
4. Maintenance or alimony payments	15.4 to 15.6
5. Subscription for venture capital trusts	15.7
6. Subscriptions for Enterprise Investment Schemes	15.8
7. Charitable covenants	15.9
8. Gift Aid payments	15.10
9. Expenses after a business has ceased	15.11
10. Losses on relevant discounted securities	15.11
11. Payments to a Trade Union or Friendly Society for death benefits	15.12

To claim any of these, enter the amounts paid and claimed in the relevant boxes.

Allowances
Figure 33 shows page 6 of the tax return.

Allowances are amounts allowed against tax, not because of any payment you have made, but because of circumstances. Everybody gets a basic personal allowance, which for 1996/97 was £3,765. Other allowances have to be claimed, and they are:

	Box
1. Blind person's allowance	16.1 to 16.2
2. Transitional allowance	16.3 to 16.4
3. Married couple's allowance	16.5 to 16.15
4. Additional personal allowance	16.16 to 16.23
5. Widow's bereavement allowance	16.24

Blind person's allowance
If you are registered as a blind person, claim this tax allowance by entering the date of registration as a blind person, and the name of the local authority with which you are registered. If you do not have enough income to use this allowance, you can ask for it to be transferred to your husband or wife.

Transitional allowance
This is an allowance which was given when separate taxation for married people was introduced. It relieved a situation where a wife was earning more than her husband. The allowance is gradually dying out, but there are a few people still claiming it. You may claim it if you satisfy the following:

- you are a married woman
- you had transitional allowance in the previous tax year
- you lived with the same husband in the previous year
- your husband was resident in the UK for the tax year
- your husband has written to his tax district asking for the relief to be given to you.

Married couple's allowance
This allowance is given to all married couples if they are living together, or, if separated, the husband is wholly maintaining his wife, and the separation is not intended to be permanent. The allowance is given to the husband unless:

- either the husband or the wife has asked for it to be shared equally, or
- both the husband and the wife have asked for it to be given entirely to the wife.

The details needed are:

- wife's full name
- date of marriage (if after 5 April 1996)
- wife's date of birth (if before 6 April 1932)
- wife's tax reference (if known).

For a married woman filling in a tax return, the details are:

- husband's full name
- date of marriage (if after 5 April 1996)
- husband's tax reference (if known).

Tick boxes 16.8, 16.10, 16.13 and 16.15 if husband and wife have agreed to share the allowance, or that the allowance should go to the wife.

If you do not have enough income to use your married allowance, you can **transfer** it to your husband or wife.

Additional personal allowance
This is an allowance given to single parents, or to married men who have to look after a child and their wife because of illness or disablement. It is given as an alternative to a married allowance (except for the case of the married man looking after children and his wife), and is the same amount as the married couple's allowance.

If the claim is made, give the details of the youngest child. If the child is 16 or over at the beginning of the tax year, give details of the child's place of education or training. If someone else shares the responsibility of looking after the child, they can agree with you who claims the allowance, or each of you can claim a percentage of the total allowance.

Widow's bereavement allowance
A widow can claim this allowance in the tax year in which her husband dies, and in the following tax year. The amount is the same as the married couple's allowance for each year. Claim this by entering the date of your husband's death.

Higher age allowances
The personal allowance and the married couple's allowance are increased when you reach the age of 65, then further increased when you reach the age of 75. These increases apply for the whole of the tax year in which you reach those ages. They are given by you completing your date of birth in box 21.4.

Other information
Figure 34 shows page 7 of the tax return.

This page asks for further information, and is the page where you calculate your own tax, if you choose to.

Tax refunds
If you have had any tax refunded to you by the tax office or the Unemployment Benefit Office, enter the amount in box 17.1.

OTHER INFORMATION for the year ended 5 April 1997

Q 17 Have you had any 1996-97 tax refunded directly by your Tax Office or Unemployment Benefit Office?　　NO ☐　YES ☐

If yes, enter the amount of the refund here

17.1 £ _____

Q 18 Do you want to calculate your tax?　　NO ☐　YES ☐

If yes do it now and then fill in boxes 18.1 to 18.9 below. Your Tax Calculation Guide will help

- Unpaid tax for earlier years included in your tax code for 1996-97　　**18.1** £ _____
- Tax due for 1996-97 included in your tax code for a later year　　**18.2** £ _____
- Total tax due for 1996-97 *(put the amount in brackets if an overpayment)*　　**18.3** £ _____
- Unpaid tax for earlier years　　**18.4** £ _____
- Overpaid tax for earlier years　　**18.5** £ _____
- Your first payment on account for 1997-98　　**18.6** £ _____

　　Tick box 18.7 if you are making a claim to reduce your payments on account and say why in the 'Additional information' box **18.7** ☐　　Tick box 18.8 if you do not need to make payments on account **18.8** ☐

- 1997-98 tax you are reclaiming now　　**18.9** £ _____

Q 19 Do you want to claim a repayment if you have paid too much tax?　　NO ☐　YES ☐

(If you tick 'No', I will set any amount you are owed against your next tax bill.)

If yes, fill in boxes 19.1 to 19.12 as appropriate

Should the repayment/payment be sent

- to you? *(tick box and go to Question 20)* **19.1** ☐

or

- your bank or building society account or other nominee *(tick box and fill in boxes 19.3 to 19.7 or boxes 19.3 to 19.12 as appropriate)*? **19.2** ☐

Please give details of your (or your nominee's) bank or building society account for repayment

Name of bank or building society **19.3** _____

Branch sort code **19.4** __ – __ – __

Account number **19.5** _____

Name of account **19.6** _____

Building society ref. **19.7** _____

Fill in boxes 19.8 to 19.12 if you want the repayment to be made to someone other than yourself (a nominee).

Name

I authorise **19.8** _____

If you want your repayment to be made to your agent tick box 19.9 **19.9** ☐

Agent's ref. for you **19.10** _____

Nominee's address **19.11** _____

Postcode _____

to receive on my behalf the amount due

This authority must be signed by you. A photocopy of your signature will not do. **19.12**

Signature _____

Q 20 Are your details on the front of the form wrong?　　NO ☐　YES ☐

If yes, please make any corrections on the front of the form

Q 21 Please give other personal details in boxes 21.1 to 21.4

Please give a daytime telephone number if convenient. It is often quicker to phone if we need to ask you about your Tax Return.

Your telephone number **21.1** _____

or, if you prefer, your agent's telephone number **21.2** _____ (also give your agent's name and reference in the 'Additional information' box on page 8)

Say if you are single, married, widowed, divorced or separated **21.3** _____

Date of birth **21.4** __ / __ / __

If you were born before 6 April 1932, or you have ticked the 'Yes' box in Question 14, or you are claiming relief for Venture Capital Trust subscriptions

TAX RETURN: PAGE 7　　　　Please turn over ➤

Fig. 34. Tax return page 7.

Tax calculation
If you want to calculate your own tax, you are now directed to the tax calculation guide, which came with the tax return and notes.

> *Warning*
> If you answer 'no' to this question, you must therefore send in the tax return before **30 September**.

USING THE TAX CALCULATION GUIDE

The tax calculation guide includes step by step instructions, and work sheets for you to use. The key steps are:

- work out your total taxable income for the year
- deduct reliefs
- deduct allowances
- work out income tax due
- add other amounts due (*eg* Class 4 National Insurance)
- add unpaid tax from earlier years
- deduct tax already paid or suffered
- work out final amount due for this tax year
- work out if you need to make payments on account for next year
- work out final amount payable.

Figure 35 shows the tax calculation guide sheets (four pages).
The work sheet supplied is for most basic cases. However, you may need a different work sheet if you had:

- any capital gains tax to pay
- lump sums or compensation payments
- gains on life assurance policies
- income from a deceased person's estate with a notional basic rate tax credit
- a refund of surplus additional voluntary contributions.

You must ask for the right work sheet.

Using the work sheets
The basic work sheet covers four pages. The first page is to bring forward your **total income** from the various supplementary pages and the main tax return. Total these to give a final figure for your income from all sources for the year. This is done by transferring the

figures from the final boxes in the supplementary pages or the main return, and the sheet tells you which boxes to use. Be careful that you transfer the right figures. When you have put all the figures in, run down the column and check them again to make sure that you have not transposed any figures (such as writing 79 instead of 97) or made any other mistakes.

On the same page, enter the **reliefs**. Again, the sheet tells you which boxes to transfer from. You must also do a calculation to 'gross up' the payments for charitable covenants and Gift Aid payments. This is because the payment is deemed to be net of basic rate tax, and the amount to deduct is the full amount. For 1996/97, therefore, what you have paid is deemed to be after deduction of tax at 24 per cent. To gross this up, multiply by 100 and then divide by 76. The reliefs are then totalled, and deducted from the total income.

Take the final figure over to the next pages, which follow through the allowances deducted, then the calculation of the tax at the different rates, and the Class 4 National Insurance. Take the final figure on this page over to the final page, and make adjustments for tax already paid at source, tax unpaid for earlier years, adjusted on your code for the current year, tax due for the current year carried forward to next year's code, and payments made on account for the current year.

The final calculation is the payment on account for the next year, which is based on the figure for the current year.

Then carry these figures to the main section of the tax return, boxes 18.1 to 18.9.

There is then a section for you to claim **repayment** if you had overpaid tax for the current year. If you do not claim repayment of overpaid tax, it will be set against the next tax bill. The boxes to use are 19.1 to 19.12.

The final sections provide **extra information**. Use them to make any corrections to details preprinted by the Inland Revenue if they are wrong (*eg* your name, address, *etc*). You may also give your telephone number, if you are happy to answer queries by telephone, in box 21.1. If you have an accountant or other agent then you may enter his or her telephone number in box 21.2. Declare your marital status in box 21.3 and your date of birth in box 21.4.

The back page of the return asks you to tick boxes and give further information if:

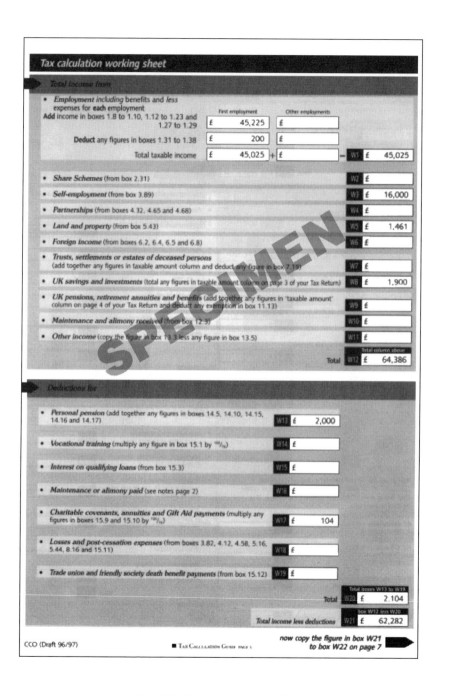

Tax calculation working sheet

Total income from

- **Employment including** benefits and **less** expenses for **each** employment
  Add income in boxes 1.8 to 1.10, 1.12 to 1.23 and 1.27 to 1.29

First employment	Other employments
£ 45,225	£

  Deduct any figures in boxes 1.31 to 1.38

  | £ 200 | £ |

  Total taxable income

  | £ 45,025 | + £ | = **W1** £ 45,025 |

- **Share Schemes** (from box 2.31) — **W2** £
- **Self-employment** (from box 3.89) — **W3** £ 16,000
- **Partnerships** (from boxes 4.32, 4.65 and 4.68) — **W4** £
- **Land and property** (from box 5.43) — **W5** £ 1,461
- **Foreign income** (from boxes 6.2, 6.4, 6.5 and 6.8) — **W6** £
- **Trusts, settlements or estates of deceased persons** (add together any figures in taxable amount column and deduct any figure in box 7.19) — **W7** £
- **UK savings and investments** (total any figures in taxable amount column on page 3 of your Tax Return) — **W8** £ 1,900
- **UK pensions, retirement annuities and benefits** (add together any figures in 'taxable amount' column on page 4 of your Tax Return and deduct any exemption in box 11.13) — **W9** £
- **Maintenance and alimony received** (from box 12.3) — **W10** £
- **Other income** (copy the figure in box 13.3 less any figure in box 13.5) — **W11** £

Total column above

Total **W12** £ 64,386

Deductions for

- **Personal pension** (add together any figures in boxes 14.5, 14.10, 14.15, 14.16 and 14.17) — **W13** £ 2,000
- **Vocational training** (multiply any figure in box 15.1 by ¹⁰⁰/₇₆) — **W14** £
- **Interest on qualifying loans** (from box 15.3) — **W15** £
- **Maintenance or alimony paid** (see notes page 2) — **W16** £
- **Charitable covenants, annuities and Gift Aid payments** (multiply any figures in boxes 15.9 and 15.10 by ¹⁰⁰/₇₆) — **W17** £ 104
- **Losses and post-cessation expenses** (from boxes 3.82, 4.12, 4.58, 5.16, 5.44, 8.16 and 15.11) — **W18** £
- **Trade union and friendly society death benefit payments** (from box 15.12) — **W19** £

Total boxes W13 to W19

Total **W20** £ 2,104

box W12 less W20

Total income less deductions **W21** £ 62,282

CCO (Draft 96/97)   ■ TAX CALCULATION GUIDE PAGE 5

now copy the figure in box W21 to box W22 on page 7 ➡

Fig. 35. Tax calculation guide.

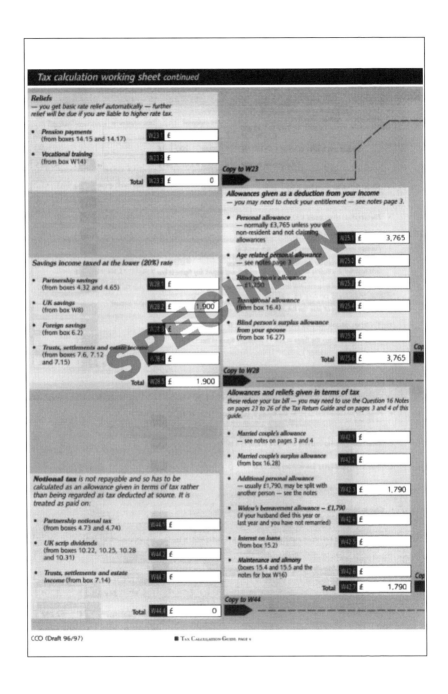

Fig. 35. Tax calculation guide (continued).

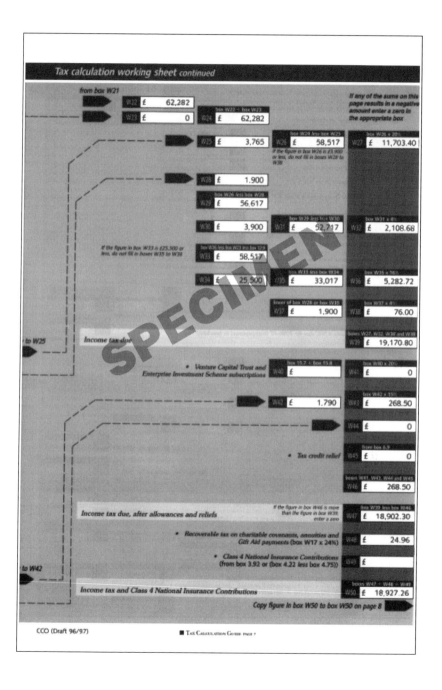

Fig. 35. Tax calculation guide (continued).

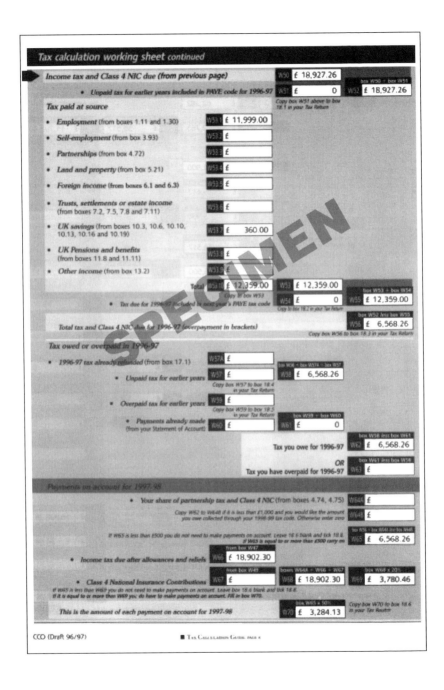

Tax calculation working sheet continued

Income tax and Class 4 NIC due (from previous page) — W50 £ 18,927.26

box W50 + box W51
W52 £ 18,927.26

• Unpaid tax for earlier years included in PAYE code for 1996-97 — W51 £ 0

Copy box W51 above to box 18.1 in your Tax Return

Tax paid at source

• Employment (from boxes 1.11 and 1.30) — W53.1 £ 11,999.00

• Self-employment (from box 3.93) — W53.2 £

• Partnerships (from box 4.72) — W53.3 £

• Land and property (from box 5.21) — W53.4 £

• Foreign income (from boxes 6.1 and 6.3) — W53.5 £

• Trusts, settlements or estate income (from boxes 7.2, 7.5, 7.8 and 7.11) — W53.6 £

• UK savings (from boxes 10.3, 10.6, 10.10, 10.13, 10.16 and 10.19) — W53.7 £ 360.00

• UK Pensions and benefits (from boxes 11.8 and 11.11) — W53.8 £

• Other income (from box 13.2) — W53.9 £

Total — W53.10 £ 12,359.00 — W53 £ 12,359.00

Copy to box W53

box W53 + box W54
W55 £ 12,359.00

• Tax due for 1996-97 included in next year's PAYE tax code — W54 £ 0

Copy to box 18.2 in your Tax Return

box W52 less box W55
W56 £ 6,568.26

Total tax and Class 4 NIC due for 1996-97 (overpayment in brackets)

Copy box W56 to box 18.3 in your Tax Return

Tax owed or overpaid in 1996-97

• 1996-97 tax already refunded (from box 17.1) — W57A £

box W56 + box W57A = box W57
W57 £

• Unpaid tax for earlier years — W57 £

box W56 + box W57A less box W57
W58 £ 6,568.26

Copy box W57 to box 18.4 in your Tax Return

• Overpaid tax for earlier years — W59 £

Copy box W59 to box 18.5 in your Tax Return

• Payments already made (from your Statement of Account) — W60 £

box W59 + box W60
W61 £ 0

box W58 less box W61
W62 £ 6,568.26

Tax you owe for 1996-97

OR

box W61 less box W58
W63 £

Tax you have overpaid for 1996-97

Payments on account for 1997-98

• Your share of partnership tax and Class 4 NIC (from boxes 4.74, 4.75) — W64A £

Copy W62 to W64B if it is less than £1,000 and you would like the amount you owe collected through your 1998-99 tax code. Otherwise enter zero — W64B £

If W65 is less than £500 you do not need to make payments on account. Leave 18.6 blank and tick 18.6. If W65 is equal to or more than £500 carry on

box W56 + box W64A less box W64B
W65 £ 6,568.26

• Income tax due after allowances and reliefs — W66 £ 18,902.30

from box W47

• Class 4 National Insurance Contributions — W67 £

from box W49

boxes W64A + W66 + W67
W68 £ 18,902.30

box W68 x 20%
W69 £ 3,780.46

If W65 is less than W69 you do not need to make payments on account. Leave 18.6 blank and tick 18.6. If it is equal to or more than W69 you do have to make payments on account. Fill in box W70.

This is the amount of each payment on account for 1997-98 — W70 £ 3,284.13

box W65 x 50%
Copy box W70 to box 18.6 in your Tax Return

Fig. 35. Tax calculation guide (continued).

		Box
1.	You expect to receive a new pension or benefit in the following tax year	22.1
2.	You do not want any tax owing to be collected through your tax code	22.2
3.	There are any estimated or provisional figures	22.3
4.	You have paid rent to a person outside the UK	22.4
5.	You claim relief now for next year's trading losses	22.5
6.	You claim to have post cessation business receipts taxed in an earlier year	22.5
7.	You claim for the 'spreading' of literary or artistic income	22.5

The **declaration** which you sign finishes off the form. It is perhaps the most important part of the form. You sign to say that the information you have given is correct and complete to the best of your knowledge and belief (box 23.1). If you sign for someone else, for example as executor, fill in box 23.2 with the detail.

Sending in the tax return
The Inland Revenue provide an envelope for you to send back the return, and the various supplementary pages, and any further lists or figures. The envelope is not postage paid, however. You must send it in to get to the Inland Revenue by 30 September if you want them to calculate your tax, otherwise by 31 January.

CHECKLIST

- Notify the Inland Revenue if you have not received a tax return.
- Read through the guide.
- Check that you have all the right pages.
- Get help sheets.
- Collect information.
- Answer questions on page 2 of the tax return.
- Fill in supplementary sheets.
- Fill in pages 3 to 8 of the tax return.
- Send tax return in – by 30 September if you want the Inland Revenue to calculate – by 31 January otherwise.
- Pay tax by 31 January.

QUESTIONS AND ANSWERS

I have not received a tax return, and I have some income which is not taxed at source. I am not sure whether I will actually have to pay any tax, since I believe that the income will be more than covered by my personal allowance. Should I ask for a tax return?

Yes. If you are not sure, get a tax return, enter the amounts, and do the calculations, or ask the Inspector of Taxes to do the calculation. If there is no tax to pay, the Inspector of Taxes will not send you a tax return next year. However, if there is some new source of income or if your income will make you taxable, the onus is still on you to ask for a tax return.

I think I have a valid claim for expenses in my job. I asked about them at the tax office, but I was told categorically that they are not allowable. What should I do?

If you think you have a valid claim, be prepared to pursue it. The rules for claiming expenses state that the expenses must be incurred 'wholly, exclusively and necessarily' for the duties performed in your employment, and that the expenses must be incurred 'in the performance of duties'. If you are uncertain about the interpretation, or about how to argue your case, you could get professional advice from an accountant.

CASE STUDIES

Anthony checks the work done

Anthony has accounts prepared by his accountant. He has kept all the details of income other than the business, and presents these to his accountant, together with his wife's tax return and her details. The accountant prepares the tax returns for both of them and presents them for their signatures, when they are in his office. Because they are signing to say that the tax returns are correct and complete, they go through the items in the tax return item by item, to satisfy themselves, before signing.

The tax return is sent off on 31 October.

Max does it himself

Max keeps his P60 from his company pension, his bank and building society interest slips, and his dividend vouchers. He also carried out some sales of shares, which produced a capital gain. He has kept all the contract notes for the sales.

He works his way through the return, completing each section in turn. Although he has carried out all the calculations himself, he sends it off on 31 August, because he does not want it hanging over him for several more months.

Yvonne gets help when needed

Yvonne has not kept her papers in good order. She asked the company accountant to sort out her tax affairs. He has got together all the papers she needed, and now she asks him if he will fill in the tax return for her. He does this, and presents it to her for signature. She has confidence in him, and wants to sign it without checking it. However, he points out that she is signing to say that it is correct and complete. He therefore makes her go through it item by item with him before she signs it. It has taken several months to get all the papers together, and it is the middle of January before it is sent off.

5
Paying the Tax

MAKING THE PAYMENTS ON ACCOUNT

From the 1996/97 tax year onwards, you may have to pay tax in **instalments**. There will be payments on account, based on the tax and Class 4 National Insurance you paid in the previous year. Then when you have assessed your tax liability for the tax year, there will be a balancing payment (or refund, if you have paid too much).

You need to distinguish between tax paid directly to the tax office and tax deducted at source. You need not make a payment on account if:

- 80 per cent or more of your total tax for the previous year was deducted at source (does not apply until 1997/98), or
- the total payments on account would be less than £500.

The payments on account consist of two half-yearly payments of exactly half the previous year's net tax liability – *ie* the total tax bill less tax deducted at source.

Example
Your tax liability for 1996/97 was £2,000, of which £200 was tax

deducted at source. You will have to pay two half-yearly payments on account of £900 each for 1997/98.

The payments are due on 31 January and 31 July. Thus the two payments on account referred to above are payable on 31 January 1998 and 31 July 1998.

You have the right to reduce or cancel the payments on account if you believe that the correct tax liability will be less, or even nil.

Payments on account are only required for income tax. They are not required for capital gains tax.

MAKING THE BALANCING PAYMENT

When you have made your own self assessment, if the tax payable is more than the amounts paid and tax deducted at source, a balancing payment is payable on the following 31 January.

Example
Following the facts in the example above, if your self assessment showed a tax liability for 1997/98 of £2,200, of which the tax deducted at source was £200, the payments would be as follows:

31 January 1998 payment on account 1997/98 tax	£900 (based on 1996/97)
31 July 1998 payment on account 1997/98 tax	£900 (based on 1996/97)
31 January 1999 balancing payment 1997/98 tax	£200
31 January 1999 payment on account 1998/99 tax	£1,000 (based on 1997/98)

The balancing payment is payable together with the first payment on account for the following year. Thus, in the above example, the total payable on 31 January 1999 is £1,200.

OFFSETTING THE BALANCING REFUND

In the same way as a balancing payment is due, a balancing refund is due if the self assessment is less than the payments on account.

Example
Following the facts in the example above, if the self assessment for 1997/98 showed a tax liability of £1,600, of which tax deducted at source was £200, the payments would be as follows:

Name

Tax reference
or
National Insurance
number

This information can be found in the top right hand corner
of your *Self Assessment Statement of Account*

Please read the explanatory notes overleaf before completing this form

I believe that

tick

- ☐   the Income Tax and Class 4 NIC payable by me for 1996-97 (net of tax deducted at source and tax credits on dividends) will be less than the payments on account due for 1996-97 based on the relevant 1995-96 income.

or

- ☐   I will not be liable to any Income Tax and Class 4 NIC in 1996-97

My reason(s)

- ☐   my business profits are less in 1996-97 than in 1995-96
- ☐   my tax allowances and reliefs are more in 1996-97 than in 1995-96
- ☐   my tax deducted at source is more in 1996-97 than in 1995-96
- ☐   **other reason, please specify**

Draft

SPECIMEN

I wish to have my payments on account for the tax year 1996-97 reduced to   £ _____   **1st payment on account.**

£ _____   **2nd payment on account.**

I understand that

- if the actual payments on account due are greater than the amounts paid, I will have to pay interest on the difference between the amounts due and the amounts paid
- any incorrect statement made fraudulently or negligently in connection with this claim could make me liable to a penalty.

Signed   Date

Please ensure that you have completed all the relevant parts of this form and signed it, otherwise your claim form will not be accepted.
You should send this form to your Tax Office.

SA303.8   22834 7.96 Niceday Stationery & Print Limited   CCO7/96   W0H2229

Fig. 36. Claim to reduce payments on account.

31 January 1998 payment on account	
1997/98 tax	£900 (based on 1996/97)
31 July 1998 payment on account	
1997/98 tax	£900 (based on 1996/97)
31 January 1999 balancing refund	
1997/98 tax	£400
31 January 1999 payment on account	
1998/99 tax	£700 (based on 1997/98)

The balancing refund of 1997/98 tax is deducted from the first payment on account of the following year, and the amount payable in this example would be £300.

ELECTING TO PAY BY PAYE

If you are an employee, you may elect to pay the balancing payment through your PAYE deductions. There are two conditions for this:

1. You must send in your tax return by 30 September following the tax year.
2. The balancing payment must not be more than £1,000.

REDUCING THE PAYMENTS ON ACCOUNT

You may reduce or cancel the payments on account if you believe that the following year's tax will be less. You must send to the Inspector of Taxes a form SA303.8 (see Figure 36).

Do not do this if the new figure you suggest is not realistic. If you do not pay enough on the payments on account, there will be an interest charge on the amount you should have paid.

Example

Following the facts in the example above, you should pay £900 for each interim payment. You make an application to reduce the interim payments to £500 each. Your self assessment for 1997/98 shows a liability of £2,200, of which the tax deducted at source is £200. You therefore pay:

31 January 1998 interim payment	
1997/98 tax	£500 (as requested)
31 July 1998 interim payment 1997/98 tax	£500 (as requested)
31 January 1999 balancing payment	
1997/98 tax	£1,000
31 January 1999 interim payment	£1,000 (based on net
1998/99 tax	1997/98 tax)

Thus, the total payment due on 31 January 1999 will be £2,000. Because the interim payments for 1997/98 should have been £900 each, there will be interest on the amount underpaid at each interim payment. In this case, the interest will be on £400 from 31 January 1998 to 31 January 1999, and on £400 from 31 July 1998 to 31 January 1999.

PAYING CAPITAL GAINS TAX

Capital gains tax is payable with the rest of your tax liability. Because capital gains tax is not necessarily due every year, the payment of capital gains tax in one year does not create a payment on account for the following year.

Example
Your tax liability for 1996/97 is £2,000, made up of income tax £1,800, and capital gains tax £200. Your payments on account for 1997/98 are:

31 January 1998 £900 (based on 1996/97 income tax)
31 July 1998   £900 (based on 1996/97 income tax)

Capital gains tax is payable on 31 January following the tax year for which it is assessed.

Example
On 31 May 1997 you sold some shares and made a gain chargeable to capital gains tax. The assessment of the capital gains tax is £500. You enter this on your tax return for the 1997/98 tax year, which you do not receive until after 5 April 1998. The capital gains tax is payable to 31 January 1999, together with income tax due on that date. There has been a delay of 1 year and 8 months between selling the shares and paying the tax.

The delay between the gain and the payment of tax could be a mixed blessing. Some people regard it as an advantage to have this long delay. Others find it too easy to forget about the tax in the meantime, and the day of reckoning comes as an unpleasant surprise.

Tip: Set aside the money to pay the tax as soon as you know how much the tax will be. If this is set aside in an account you would not otherwise draw on, it is always there when needed.

CHECKING YOUR STATEMENT

From the 1996/97 year, all taxpayers received **itemised statements** of their account with the Inland Revenue. These statements are rather like credit card statements. An example is shown in Figure 37. The statement shows any amounts owing from you, and a notice to pay the next amount of tax due from you. A tear off slip at the bottom of the statement is provided for you to pay the amount through a bank giro credit or, if you prefer, to send with your cheque to the Collector of Taxes.

They show the amounts due from you, and the amounts you have paid. If you have paid late, there will be an automatic charge for interest, in the same way as a credit card statement. If the interest charge has not been paid, it continues to attract further interest until it has been paid off.

Therefore, whenever you receive a statement, check what is on it. You should be able to check any tax due from the copies of your tax return. If there are any entries for penalties or surcharges, you should also have been told about these by the Inland Revenue. Check also that the amounts due from you are shown with their correct dates.

Then check the amounts and dates of payments you have made. If there appears to be any undue delay between your making the payment and the date it was received by the Collector of Taxes, you should investigate this.

PAYING ON TIME

It is important to pay the tax on time. **Interest** is automatically charged to your statement for any late payment. In addition, there are **surcharges** to encourage prompt payment. If tax is still unpaid after 28 days from the due date, a surcharge of five per cent of the tax is charged. If the payment is more than six months late, a further five per cent of the tax is charged.

You may appeal against a surcharge, but you must be able to show a 'reasonable excuse' for late payment. Each case is considered on its own merits in deciding what is a 'reasonable excuse'. Inability to pay is never allowed as a reasonable excuse.

It may seem an obvious point, but do not leave your tax return until the very last minute. This may be a temptation – the tax return is due by 31 January following the tax year, and payment is due on the same date. But it is all too easy to do this, and find that there is

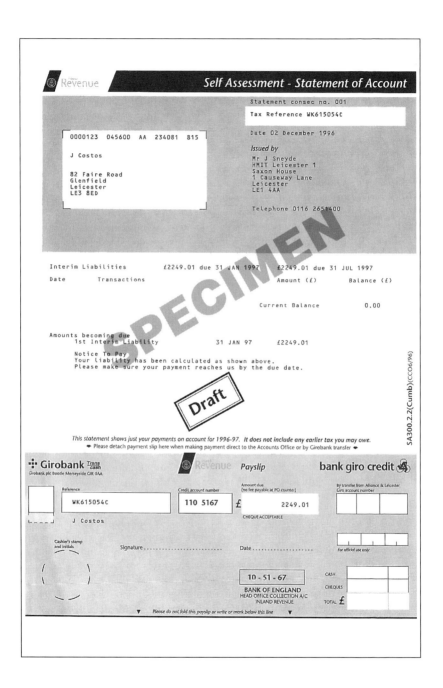

Fig. 37. Inland Revenue statement of account.

some last minute hitch. The tax return is not sent in on time, and the tax is not paid on time. The interest charge is automatic.

CHECKLIST

- Payment on account dates:
  - 31 January in the tax year
  - 31 July following the tax year.

- Balancing payment date:
  - 31 January following the tax year.

- Capital gains tax included in the balancing payment due:
  - 31 January following the tax year.

- Summary of payment dates:
  - 31 January 1997 – first payment on account for 1996/97
  - 31 July 1997 – second payment on account for 1996/97
  - 31 January 1998 – balancing payment for 1996/97 including any capital gains tax (or balancing repayment)
    - first payment on account for 1997/98
  - 31 July 1998 – second payment on account for 1997/98
  - 31 January 1999 – balancing payment for 1997/98 including any capital gains tax (or balancing repayment)
    - first payment on account for 1998/99.

QUESTIONS AND ANSWERS

I have received a statement showing that I paid an amount to the Inland Revenue on 21 February, but on checking I find that the cheque stub shows I wrote the cheque on 28 January. What should I do?

Write to the tax office that issued the statement and explain the situation. Ask that the payment date be re-assigned, and if there are any interest charges triggered by the alleged late payment, ask for them to be cancelled.

I am not sure about my tax liability for the current year compared with the previous year. It could be more or less. Should I apply to reduce the interim payment?

No. If there is any doubt, and you can afford it, pay the original amount demanded. If you reduce it too much, you run the risk of incurring an interest charge. If it turns out that your liability for the year is less than the payments on account you made, the Inland Revenue will pay interest on the tax refunded.

CASE STUDIES

Anthony reduces the payment on account

Anthony's 1996/97 tax bill on his self employment income was £2,500, made up of tax £2,100 and Class 4 National Insurance £400. His payments on account are assessed at £1,250 each half year, 31 January 1998 and 31 July 1998.

However, he was late in paying the January payment on account, and did not pay it until 28 February. He received a statement for interest in March, which he paid to stop further interest running.

By June, however, he realised that he was not going to make as much profit as the previous year. He therefore applied to reduce the payments on account to £1,000 each. Having already paid £1,250, he pays £750 in July.

When he made his self assessment, the final figure of tax and Class 4 National Insurance came to £1,900 for the year. Therefore, he had overpaid on his payments on account by £100, and this balancing refund is to be deducted from the first payment on account of 1998/99 tax. The first payment on account for 1998/99 is £950, being half the 1997/98 tax bill. Thus, the amount he has to pay is £850.

Max pays by PAYE

Max had a tax bill for 1996/97 of £1,400. He paid the two payments on account of £700 each for 1997/98. When he made his self assessment for 1997/98, the final tax bill was £1,600. He therefore owed £200 extra. However, he sent his return and self assessment in before 30 September, and elected to pay the amount due by the PAYE system. His code number for 1998/99 was therefore adjusted to take this into account.

Yvonne pays penalty surcharge and interest

Yvonne has a tax bill for 1996/97 of £300 on her property income. No payments on account were needed, the total being under £500. Due to pressure of work, she did not get her tax return in until March 1998. At the same time as sending it in, she paid the amount she had calculated in her self assessment, of £400 for the balancing payment for 1997/98.

However, because the tax return was late, she incurred an automatic penalty of £100, and because the tax was paid late there is an interest charge and a surcharge of £20 (five per cent of the tax due). She received a statement at the end of March showing the penalty, interest and surcharge, but again overlooked it. At the end of the next month, she received a further statement with further interest on the balance of the previous statement. She finally paid this amount, to stop any further interest mounting up.

DISCUSSION POINTS

1. How would you know if your tax assessment for the coming year was likely to be less than the previous year? Is your record keeping adequate, and up to date enough to allow you to do this?

2. Have you arranged your finances so that you have access to adequate funds when the tax payments are due?

3. Do you set aside a 'tax provision' in a separate account? If so, are you self disciplined enough not to draw on it for other purposes?

6
Correcting Mistakes

AMENDING ENTRIES

After you have sent in your tax return, you may find that you have made a mistake of some sort. It may have been omitting to enter something, an adding up error – any sort of mistake.

You may amend your tax return by writing to the Inspector of Taxes at any time up to one year from the normal filing date. You may not do this if your return has already been chosen for an enquiry.

Receiving notice of correction from the Inland Revenue

The Inspector of Taxes can also correct any obvious mistakes in your return. For example, if you have carried a wrong figure from one box to another box in the form, it will be corrected by this process. There are two conditions to this:

1. The Inspector of Taxes must do this within nine months of receiving your return.
2. The Inspector of Taxes must notify you of the corrections.

If this happens, the Inspector of Taxes will write to you, and tell you about the correction that has been made. He will also tell you of any revised amount you have to pay.

MAKING AN 'ERROR OR MISTAKE' CLAIM

There are provisions in the Taxes Acts for you to make claims if you believe that you have made a mistake on your tax returns. These claims may be made within a time limit of up to five years from 31 January following the end of the tax year. You simply write to the Inspector of Taxes telling him about the mistake, and asking for amendments to be made to your tax assessments.

RECEIVING NOTICE OF AN INLAND REVENUE ENQUIRY

The Inland Revenue may make an enquiry into your tax return at any time before the end of the twelve months from the normal filing date for a tax return, or longer if you sent your tax return in late. This is dealt with in more detail in the next chapter.

In normal circumstances this means that unless a tax return is amended by you or the Inspector of Taxes, it is considered as final and conclusive twelve months after the normal filing date.

CASE STUDIES

Anthony omits to claim for relief
Anthony sends in his tax return, but realises within a month that he has omitted to include the claim for his pension premium payments. He writes to the Inspector of Taxes telling him the amount of the claim that has been omitted. The Inspector of Taxes amends the entries and calculates the new amount of tax.

As Anthony has already paid, he gets a repayment of tax overpaid.

Max transposes figures
Max has sent his tax return in, but incorrectly carried one figure from the tax return to the calculation working sheet. He had tax of £2,140 deducted from his pension by PAYE. However, he carried this to the calculation working sheet at £2,410. This meant that he

had underpaid tax by £270.

The Inspector of Taxes writes to him to tell him about the mistake, and to request the additional payment of £270.

7
Surviving an
Inland Revenue Enquiry

RECEIVING THE NOTIFICATION

At any time up to a year from the filing date (31 January following
the year end) the Inland Revenue have the right to enquire into the
completeness and accuracy of your tax return. If you have submitted
your tax return late, they have one year from the quarter day
following the date you actually sent it in. These quarter dates are 31
January, 30 April, 31 July and 31 October.

Therefore, if you sent your return in on 15 February, they have
until 30 April next year to open an enquiry.

The Inspector of Taxes will choose some taxpayers for enquiry.
Most are chosen on the basis that tax is thought to be at risk,
because there is some anomaly or the computer has suggested there
may be a reason to enquire. However, a small proportion will be
chosen at random.

The first thing you will receive is a letter from the Inspector of
Taxes asking for more information or explanations. He may also
issue a formal notice requiring you to provide documents, records,
accounts *etc* relating to the return.

SUPPLYING THE INFORMATION

When you receive a request from the Inspector of Taxes for more information, provided it has been sent in the time limit mentioned above, you have no right to challenge his right to enquire into your tax return.

Send the information asked for as promptly as possible. Answer all the questions raised, but do not try to go further than the points raised by the Inspector of Taxes.

Warning

If you are aware of any mistake, or anything you have not declared, make a full disclosure straight away. If there is a later settlement, including penalties, the penalties will be less if you have co-operated as early as possible.

When you have sent the information to the Inspector of Taxes, this may lead to further questions. Continue to answer all relevant questions. You do, however, have the right to appeal on the grounds that the questions or information asked for are not relevant in deciding whether your return is complete and correct.

ATTENDING INTERVIEWS

The enquiries may reach a point where the Inspector of Taxes feels it would be better to see you. You may also feel this would be better and help clear up the enquiry more quickly. If you suggest this, your Inspector of Taxes will probably agree – he wants to clear it up quickly as much as you do.

The interview will normally be at his office. If you have a good reason, though, he may agree to meet you at your house or business. The reason would normally be that you are unable to travel to his office through incapacity or some other cause.

When you are at the interview, remember three basic rules:

- always remain courteous

- if you want to make any disclosures, make them straight away, otherwise –

- just answer the questions – don't volunteer any further information.

At an interview, the Inspector of Taxes wants to clear up the enquiry as far as possible. Be prepared to discuss a settlement figure if there is any tax under-declared.

KNOWING YOUR RIGHTS

You have no control over the Inspector of Taxes' right to choose your tax return for enquiry. However, you do have certain rights during the course of the enquiry. These are the Inspector of Taxes' rights and your rights.

The Inspector of Taxes' rights

Your rights

The Inspector of Taxes has the right to enquire into the completeness and accuracy of any person's tax return.

The Inspector of Taxes must notify you within the time limits that your tax return is chosen for enquiry. If you have sent in your tax return by the deadline filing date (31 January following receipt of the tax return) then he has until 31 January next year. Thus, if you sent in your 1997 return on 30 June 1997, the deadline date is 31 January 1998, and the Inspector of Taxes has until 31 January 1999 to send the notice of enquiry.

If you sent in your tax return late, he has until the quarter day following the anniversary of the day you sent your return.

If you sent in your 1997 tax return on 2 February 1998, the Inspector of Taxes has until 30 April 1999 to send the notice.

If the Inspector of Taxes has not sent you the notice by the due date, he has lost the right to enquire into your tax return for that year.

The Inspector of Taxes has the right to demand that you produce any documents or other particulars relevant to that return.

The Inspector of Taxes must specify a time limit for you to produce the documents, and the time limit must not be less than 30 days.

You have the right to appeal against the notice demanding documents, but only on two grounds:
1. Whether the information demanded is relevant.
2. Whether you have been given enough time to appeal.

The Commissioners can confirm all or part of the notice. If they agree with you, they can set it aside. If they do confirm all or part of the notice, you then have 30 days to comply with it.

You have no right of appeal against the Commissioners' decision.

If you do not produce the items requested, there is an initial fine of £50. Then the Inland Revenue can impose further fines of £30 per day for any further delay.

You may appeal against the penalty.

However, if the Commissioners impose a fine for this offence, as part of formal penalty proceedings, it can be up to £150 per day.

You may apply to the Commissioners at any time in the course of an enquiry to close it down. If they agree with you that there are no reasonable grounds for continuing the enquiry, they will issue a notice to the Inspector of Taxes stating that the enquiry should be ended.

When an enquiry is ended, the Inspector of Taxes must issue you with a notice confirming that the enquiry is ended.

CLOSING DOWN THE ENQUIRY

When you and the Inspector of Taxes agree that all the enquiries are completed, or when the Commissioners issue a notice that the Inspector of Taxes must close the enquiry down, then the Inspector of Taxes will issue you with a notice confirming that the enquiry is ended. He will also tell you if there are any adjustments to make to your self assessment, if there are any under-declarations of tax – or indeed if there are any over-declarations.

You then have 30 days to amend your self assessment. You may also, however, take the opportunity to revise any claims you have previously made, whether in the original return or in the course of the enquiry.

AGREEING THE SETTLEMENT

If the Inspector of Taxes has discovered that additional tax is due, and that you have not disclosed all the facts, he may seek a contract settlement, including interest, if any of the tax should have been paid on a past date. The settlement may also include penalties. As already shown, there are fixed penalties for offences such as failing to comply with demands to supply information or documents, but there is also a penalty geared to the amount of the tax under-declared.

This tax-geared penalty starts at 100 per cent of the tax under-declared, but is then reduced for different elements. These elements include:

- disclosure – *ie* whether you have voluntarily disclosed information to the Inspector of Taxes

- degree of co-operation

- size and gravity of the case.

In theory, if all of these elements were fully in your favour, then the penalty would be reduced to nil. If you think that the penalty has been too harsh, considering your conduct of the enquiry, you may challenge the calculation of the penalty.

When all is finally agreed, you will be asked to sign a statement of full disclosure, and a statement of assets. The statement of full disclosure certifies that you have disclosed to the Inspector of Taxes all the facts that are relevant to the calculation of your tax for the period covered by the enquiry.

The statement of assets shows all your private and business assets, and all your private and business liabilities.

CHECKLIST

- Notice of enquiry sent by Inspector of Taxes.
- Request for information.
- Attend interviews.
- Know your rights.
- Close the enquiry.
- Agree the settlement (if any).

CASE STUDIES

Anthony agrees to an adjustment

Anthony's accountant receives a notice that Anthony's tax return has been selected for enquiry because the Inspector of Taxes believes that the rate of profit shown in the accounts is low compared with similar businesses. The Inspector of Taxes asks to see the business records from which his accounts have been prepared, and the building society statements and share dividend vouchers.

All the documents are sent to the Inspector of Taxes. After protracted correspondence, and an interview, Anthony agrees an increased profit figure to be self assessed, due to insufficient allowance for his private use of the business telephone and car. The increased figure is £500. When Anthony amends his self assessment, the time limit for making a carry back claim has not passed, so he also makes a claim to carry back a further £500 of pension premium relief from the following year. This relief is set off against the additional £500 due. There is therefore no additional tax to pay.

Max is randomly selected for enquiry

Max receives a notice that his tax return has been selected for enquiry. This is on a random basis. The Inspector of Taxes requests sight of all the documents including Max's personal bank statements. Max is upset by this request, and is advised that he can appeal to the Commissioners. He does this, but the Commissioners decide that all the information requested, including the bank statements, is relevant to his tax return. He therefore complies with the request.

The Inspector of Taxes asks further questions about some of the entries on his bank statements and building society accounts. Max cannot recall all of these items, becomes further alarmed, and goes to see an accountant. The accountant helps him through the enquiry, and accompanies him to an interview with the Inspector of Taxes.

In the end, all the enquiries are satisfactorily answered. The Inspector of Taxes issues a notice that the enquiry has ended, and there is no further tax to pay. However, Max has to pay the accountant's charges. He feels that he should have some claim on the Inland Revenue for this, since he only engaged the accountant because of the enquiry, and in the end no extra tax was payable. However, he is not able to claim anything against the Inland Revenue for this.

Yvonne forgets about her rental income

Yvonne receives a notice that her tax return has been chosen for enquiry. She is not sure why this is, and duly sends along all the information she used to complete the return. However, she has forgotten about the rents from her property. This is the first tax year after she inherited the property, and she had used last year's tax return as her guide.

The Inspector of Taxes is aware of the property, and is therefore surprised that she has not declared the rents, or sent in any details about them with the information he requested. He asks her to think again about any sources of income. She still cannot think what the omitted source of income might be, and the Inspector of Taxes has to prompt her.

She finally realises, and sends the Inspector of Taxes all the information about the income from the property. No other omissions are found. The Inspector of Taxes accepts the reason for the oversight, but still contends that it amounted to negligence. In the end, after negotiating the figure, Yvonne accepts a penalty of ten per cent of the tax due.

DISCUSSION POINTS

1. If you received an enquiry from the Inspector of Taxes suggesting that there might be an omission from your tax return, how would you be able to check through all your tax return entries?

2. How would you handle the enquiry, attend an interview, deal with the questions? At what point would you feel you needed outside help?

8
Getting Help

ENGAGING AN ACCOUNTANT

Should you use an accountant? (The term 'accountant' is used here to include tax practitioners who are not qualified professionally.)

If your affairs are relatively simple, and you do not have any income other than your salary, you are not likely to need an accountant. If your affairs are any more complicated, then an accountant is likely to be useful. If you are self employed, it is more than likely that you have an accountant already – something like three-quarters of all self employed people use an accountant of some sort.

If you have:

- expenses against your employment of any consequence
- benefits in kind or expenses in your employment
- share options
- income from property
- foreign income
- income from a trust or estate
- claims for non-resident status.
- capital gains
- investment income
- stocks and shares
- unit trusts

then it is likely that an accountant will be of use to you.

Some people are happy to engage an accountant to offload the detailed work involved. Some see tax returns as a worry and a headache, and are willing to pay for that to be taken away from them. Some will recognise their affairs are complex, and engage an accountant for the peace of mind of knowing that all angles will be taken care of, and everything is done properly.

Others recognise that their tax burden is relatively heavy, and seek to plan their affairs so as to minimise their tax burden within the law.

Qualified or not?

A qualified accountant is one who belongs to a professional body, such as the Institute of Chartered Accountants or the Chartered Association of Certified Accountants. Only members of these bodies are allowed to call themselves 'Chartered Accountants' or 'Certified Accountants' respectively. There is no restriction on the use of the word 'Accountant'. Anyone may describe himself as an accountant.

If you are seeking the help of an accountant, should you go to a qualified accountant, or not?

A qualified accountant will probably be more expensive than an unqualified accountant. A qualified accountant, however, has gone through a rigorous period of training, and must continue to undergo training and education after he has qualified. He is subject to strict regulatory and disciplinary procedures from his Institute or Association.

USING THE INLAND REVENUE'S HELP

The Inland Revenue do not wish you to pay any more tax than is necessary. They are willing to help you if you do not understand any parts of the form.

The guide that comes with the tax return tries to explain the form, and to help you step by step through the return.

Asking for help sheets

If you need any more help, you can request help sheets on various subjects. There are over 50 help sheets listed in the tax return guide, and these cover a wide variety of subjects. They cover in rather more detail some aspects of your tax affairs which are not straightforward. For instance, the 'Employment' section of the tax return lists

the following help sheets:
- vouchers, credit cards and tokens
- living accommodation
- motor mileage and car allowances
- lump sums and compensation payments
- foreign earnings deductions
- capital allowances
- non-taxable payments or benefits for employees
- payslips and coding notices
- mobile telephones
- assets provided by the employer for private use
- employment – residence and domicile issues
- payments in kind.

Asking for help

If you need any more help, you may telephone or visit your local tax office, whose address and telephone number appear on your tax return. Alternatively, there is a Helpline telephone number on your tax return, which is open longer hours than the tax offices.

Remember though that if you have any matter you wish to argue or dispute, or a grey area, the Inland Revenue will not necessarily 'take your side'. Although they want to help you, their job is to collect tax from you. If you are confident that you have a good case in, say, claiming for an expense to be allowable, be prepared to argue your side of the case. This is the sort of area where an accountant is likely to have some experience and access to information about cases that have been decided in the past.

Getting the Inland Revenue to do the calculations

If you send your tax return in by 30 September, the Inspector of Taxes will carry out the tax calculations. This is a limited service, however. You must have filled in all the relevant parts of the tax return to declare your income. All that they will do is the mathematical calculation of the tax due, and tell you how much it is.

Even though the Inspector of Taxes does this, he is doing it as your agent. The tax calculation is still your own self assessment.

The Taxpayers Charter

For some years now, the Inland Revenue have operated under this charter. It states:

'You are entitled to expect the Inland Revenue:

'To be fair

- by settling your tax affairs impartially
- by expecting you to pay only what is due under the law
- by treating everyone with equal fairness.

'To help you

- to get your tax affairs right
- to understand your rights and obligations
- by providing clear leaflets and forms
- by giving you information and assistance at our enquiry offices
- by being courteous at all times.

'To provide an efficient service

- by settling your tax affairs promptly and accurately
- by keeping your private affairs strictly confidential
- by using the information you give us only as allowed by the law
- by keeping to a minimum your costs of complying with the law
- by keeping our costs down.

'To be accountable for what we do

- by setting standards for ourselves and publishing how well we live up to them.

'If you are not satisfied

- we will tell you exactly how to complain
- you can ask for your tax affairs to be looked at again
- you can appeal to an independent tribunal
- your MP can refer your complaint to the Ombudsman.

'In return we need you
- to be honest
- to give us accurate information.'

CASE STUDIES

Anthony uses an accountant
Anthony has always used an accountant to prepare his accounts and to deal with his tax work. He sees no reason to change for the self assessment regime. He feels that, although the accountant's fees are

not small, he is willing to pay for the peace of mind, and the help his accountant gives him in running his business and dealing with complying with the law in all sorts of ways.

Max gets help from the Inland Revenue when needed

Max has always felt capable of dealing with his own tax affairs. He did ask for professional help when the Inland Revenue enquired into his tax return. However, that incurred a fee which he was not able to recover from the Inland Revenue. He feels that he will deal with his own affairs, and seek help from the Inland Revenue when necessary. He hopes that he will not be selected for an enquiry again, and therefore he should not need professional help again.

Yvonne gets help from a colleague

Yvonne needed some help in getting her affairs in order, and she asked the company accountant. He helped her, but she realised that the real problem lay in her ability to keep her affairs tidy and in order. She will try to be more methodical in future, but she feels that she will probably need help again.

DISCUSSION POINTS

1. Do you feel that if you approached the Inland Revenue for help, you would be opening the door to an enquiry? If so, do you feel that this lack of trust is well founded?

2. How would you know when your affairs are complex enough to need outside help?

9
Avoiding Penalties, Interest and Surcharges

KEEPING TO DEADLINES

The most important deadline is the filing date for the tax return. If you want the Inspector of Taxes to carry out the calculations, you must get the return in by the later of:

- 30 September after the end of the tax year, or
- two months after the tax return has been issued to you.

If you miss this deadline, there is no penalty, but you must do your own calculations. The final deadline is the later of:

- 31 January after the end of the tax year, or
- three months after the tax return has been issued to you.

If the tax return is sent in late, there is an automatic penalty of £100. If it is more than six months late, the further penalty is £200, or the Inspector of Taxes may ask the Commissioners to apply a further penalty of £60 per day after the Commissioners have directed that the tax return must be sent in. The Inland Revenue have stated that they will only seek to apply this penalty when they believe that the tax at risk is believed to be high.

If the tax return is still not sent in a year after the filing date, a further penalty of up to 100 per cent of the tax liability for the year is imposed.

The total of all the penalties is limited to the amount of the tax due.

You are allowed to appeal to the Commissioners against the penalties. They may set aside a penalty if you can show that you had a reasonable excuse for the delay. The reasonable excuse must have applied throughout the whole period of failure, not just for a part of the period.

Determination

If you have not sent in your tax return, the Inland Revenue have the right to make a 'determination' of the amount of Income Tax and Capital Gains Tax due from you. They must do this within five years of the original filing date. They will do this 'to the best of their information and belief'. **There is no right of appeal against this determination**. It is treated as your self assessment. The only way to overturn it is to send in your tax return with your self assessment of tax. Once the determination has been made, you must send in your tax return by the later of:

- five years from the original filing date or
- twelve months of the determination.

PAYING TAX ON TIME

Interest

Interest is charged on all late payments. This applies to payments of tax on account, the balancing tax, interest, penalties and surcharges. Interest is charged at the 'official rate' which is geared to prevailing bank interest rates. The list of the official rates of interest, and the dates for which they applied, are available from your local tax office.

Surcharges

The addition to interest on late paid tax, the following surcharges are added:

Tax paid after 28 days of due date, but not later than 6 months – 5% of tax due.

Tax paid more than 6 months after the due date – 10% of tax due.

Appeals are allowed against the surcharges, but not against the interest. To set aside the surcharge, you must show a reasonable excuse for late payment – but inability to pay is *not* accepted as a reasonable excuse.

Surcharges do not apply to payments on account, only to final payments of tax and Class 4 National Insurance. A surcharge cannot be made in addition to a tax geared penalty.

MEETING ALL YOUR OBLIGATIONS

There are penalties for various other failures.

Record keeping
The Inland Revenue may impose a penalty of up to £3,000 for each failure to keep or preserve adequate records for the required time in support of a return. However, there is a right of appeal against this, and the Inland Revenue have said that they will only seek to apply this maximum penalty in the most extreme of cases.

Enquiries
In the course of an enquiry, if the Inland Revenue have issued a notice requiring production of documents, failure to comply incurs a penalty of £50, with a further penalty of £30 per day for any further delay. This is the maximum that the Inland Revenue can impose, but if the Commissioners impose a penalty for this failure, as part of formal penalty proceedings, the maximum penalty is £150 per day.

CHECKLIST

Penalties

Late delivery of tax return (up to six months late)	£100 automatic fine
Late delivery of tax return (more than six months late)	a further £100 automatic fine
Late delivery of tax return (more than one year late)	up to 100% of tax due
Delay after Commissioners direct tax return to be sent	£60 per day
Failure to keep and retain proper records	up to £3,000 for each failure
Failure to produce records requested by the Inspector of Taxes in the course of an enquiry	£50, plus £30 per day
Failure to produce records requested in the course of an enquiry – penalty issued by Commissioners	up to £150 per day

Surcharges

Tax paid between 28 days and six months late	5% of tax due
Tax paid more than six months late	10% of tax due

Interest

Charged on all late payments	Interest at the official published rate

10
Paying Less Tax

USING YOUR ALLOWANCES

Everyone has a basic tax allowance which for 1996/97 was £3,765. You are only taxed on any income above that figure. You do not have to claim this allowance specially. It is given to you as a right.

However, other allowances have to be claimed. This is done, as we saw in Chapter 4, on page 6 of the tax return. Therefore, do make sure that you claim all the allowances to which you are entitled. To recap, these include:

- Blind Person's Allowance
- Transitional Allowance
- Married Couple's Allowance
- Additional Personal Allowance
- Widow's Bereavement Allowance
- Transfer of Surplus Allowances.

If you are in any doubt as to whether you might qualify for any of these allowances, go back to Chapter 4 and check.

Apart from the obvious precaution of making sure you claim all that you are entitled to, you can use the allowances to reduce your tax bill. This opportunity arises especially for married couples. The general principle is to equalise your income as far as possible. This is only possible, of course, where you have control over the income. For example, if the only income of a couple is the salary that the husband earns, it is not possible to do anything about that.

However, if there is also some money in a building society earning interest, you do have control over that. (See Example 1 below.)

Businesses
The same principle could be put to work if one partner has a business. If, for example, a husband has a business, he could pay a salary to his wife. If the wife has a personal allowance as yet unused, she would have no tax liability, and her salary would reduce her husband's taxable profits, and also his Class 4 National Insurance liability.

If you wish to do this, however, there are two things to note.

1. The work actually done by the wife for the husband's business must be enough to justify her salary.

2. The salary must actually be paid to her.

A husband has a salary of £10,000 a year. He also has a building society account earning interest of £1,000 per year. His wife has no income. The tax saving could be:

	Present position	If the building society account were transferred to the wife	
		Husband	Wife
	£	£	£
Salary	10,000	10,000	
Interest	1,000		1,000
Total income	11,000		
Personal allowance	3,765	3,765	3,765
Taxable	7,235	6,235	NIL
Tax due			
£3,900 x 20% (lower rate)	780.00	780.00	
£1,000 x 20% (interest)	200.00		
£2,335 x 24%	560.40	560.40	
	1,540.40	1,340.40	
Married couple's allowance	268.50	268.50	
Total tax	1,271.90	1,071.90	
Tax saving £200			

Example 1.

This can be taken a stage further. There are many situations in which a business is run, not by the husband on his own, but by the husband and wife together. In these circumstances, there is no reason why the business may not be made into a partnership between husband and wife. The profits can be shared in whatever proportion you decide (not necessarily equally) and full use can be made of the tax allowances, and the Class 4 National Insurance allowances.

Once again, you must ensure that a partnership for tax purposes does reflect the commercial reality. The wife must actually have all the duties and responsibilities of a partner. She must, for instance, be able to order goods from suppliers. Her name must be on the business bank account. If the business is VAT registered, that registration must be in the name of the partnership.

Capital allowances
Capital allowances are given on assets used for a business (or for assets used in earning a salary). However, the capital allowances do not have to be claimed, or even if claimed, they do not have to be claimed in full. If the personal allowance is not fully used up, capital allowances may be disclaimed or claimed in part. There is, of course, no advantage to claiming further allowances if the tax bill is already nil. (See Example 2.)

You are a married person and have business profits of £5,500, and you can claim capital allowances on assets with a value of £3,000.

	If you claimed full allowances:	*If capital allowance claim limited to £483:*
	£	£
Profits	5,500.00	5,500.00
Capital allowance – 25% x 3,000	750.00	483.00
Net amount	4750.00	5017.00
Personal allowance	3675.00	3675.00
Taxable	1075.00	1342.00
Tax due at 20%	215.00	268.40
Married couple's allowance	268.50	268.50
Tax	NIL	NIL
Capital allowance carried forward	2,250.00	2,517.00

The tax bill is still nil, but there is now a larger amount to carry forward for capital allowances to be claimed in future years.

Example 2.

The husband has a salary of £35,000, and some property income of £5,000. The wife has a salary of £6,000. The tax position is:

	Present position		If the property were transferred to the wife	
	Husband £	Wife £	Husband £	Wife £
Salary	35,000	6,000	35,000	6,000
Property income	5,000			5,000
Total income	40,000			11,000
Personal allowance	3,765	3,765	3,765	3,765
Taxable	36,235	2,235	31,235	7,235
Tax due				
20% x 3,900	780.00	447.00	780.00	780.00
24% x 21,600	5184.00		5,184.00	800.40
40% x 10,735	4,294.00		2,294.00	
	10,258.00		8,258.00	1,580.40
Married couple's allowance	268.50		268.50	
	9,989.50	447.00	7,989.50	1,580.40
Total tax		10,436.50		9,569.90
Tax saving £866.60				

Example 3.

Using the tax bands

Tax is charged at different rates. For 1996/97, the first £3,900 of taxable income is taxed at 20 per cent, the next £21,600 at 24 per cent, and the rest at 40 per cent. The lower rate tax bands can be regarded as a sort of allowance. Therefore, if there is any possibility of equalising incomes as far as possible between husband and wife, it saves tax to be able to transfer some income from a partner who pays tax at 40 per cent to the other who pays tax at a lower rate. (See Example 3.)

Sharing the married couple's allowance

We saw when filling in the tax return that the married couple's allowance may be shared between both partners or allocated to one of them. What are the circumstances in which these options might be considered?

The overall principle again is to equalise incomes as far as possible between husband and wife. However, the married couple's allowance is given at 15 per cent only – it is not given as a relief at the highest rate of tax you bear. Therefore, the only occasion in which it is useful to vary the allocation of it is when one partner is not taxable at all, or if the allowance (£1,790 at 15% = £268.50) would be more than his or her tax liability.

It is possible to transfer any surplus married couple's allowance not used to the other partner. This is not done automatically. You have to sign an election form to do this.

Age allowance restriction

If you are over 65, you are entitled to a higher personal allowance – for 1996/97 this was £4,910 instead of the normal personal allowance of £3,765. If you are over 75, this allowance increases further to £5,090. You are also entitled to a higher married couple's allowance of £3,115, or £3,155 if you are over 75. This allowance depends on the age of the elder of the two partners.

However, the personal and married couple's allowance are restricted if your income is over a certain amount. For 1996/97, the limit for this purpose was £15,200. Your higher allowance is restricted by half the amount by which your income exceeds that limit. The allowance cannot be restricted to less than the normal personal allowance, though.

Examples

1. You are aged 70, and your total income is £16,000. The excess of your income over the limit is £800, so your allowance is restricted by £400. Thus, the allowance is £4,910 less £400 – £4,510.

2. You are aged 76 and your total income is £18,200. The excess of your income over the limit is £3,000, so the restriction would be £1,500. However, this would bring the higher age allowance of £5,090 down to £3,590. This figure is less than the normal allowance of £3,765. Your allowance is therefore £3,765.

How can this be used to reduce your tax bill?

If your income is over the limit for restricting the higher allowance, but your wife or your husband's income is not, then if you could transfer some income to your wife or husband, it would reduce your tax bill. (See Example 4, page 143).

Mr and Mrs X are both over 65, but under 75. They have the following incomes:

Husband	£
Pensions	15,000
Investment income	1,000
Property income	1,500

Wife	£
Pension	3,000
Investment income	1,000

Their tax bill could be reduced if the investment income and the property income were transferred to the wife.

	Present position		If investment income and property income were transferred to wife	
	Husband	Wife	Husband	Wife
	£	£	£	£
Pensions	15,000	3,000	15,000	3,000
Investment income	1,000	1,000		2,000
Property income	1,500			1,500
	17,500	4,000	15,000	6,500

Age allowance				
restriction	4,910		4,910	4,910	4,910
Income	17,500			
Limit	15,200			
Excess	2,300			
Half	1,150			
Restricted allowance 3,760				
Minimum allowance		3,765		
Taxable		13,735	NIL	10,090	1,590

Tax due				
20% x 3,900	780.00		780.00	318.00
20% x 1,000	200.00			
24% x 8,835	2121.40		1,485.60	
	3,101.40		2,265.60	318.00

Married couple's allowance				
Age allowance				
3,115 x 15%	467.25		467.25	
			1,798.35	318.00
Total tax bill	2,634.15		2,116.35	

There has been a tax saving of £517.80

Example 4.

USING YOUR RELIEFS

We saw the reliefs in detail when filling in the tax return.

Pension premiums

Perhaps the most significant relief available is the personal pension relief or retirement annuity relief. If you have qualifying earnings either from self employment or from employment, then putting money into a pension scheme is one of the best and most tax efficient forms of investment. You will receive tax relief at your highest rate on the premiums, and the money invested in your pension fund also grows free of tax. When the pension policy matures, you have the opportunity to take the full pension or a reduced pension and a tax free lump sum up to a certain limit.

When paying pension premiums, make sure that you only enter into a regular commitment for monthly or annual premiums for an amount that you can comfortably afford. It is possible to pay by way of a single premium into a pension policy. This can be the most beneficial way to make use of this for tax planning purposes.

Carry back and carry forward

You can make use of the facility to carry forward unused relief or to carry back premiums. This can be very useful if you have one tax year when you are in a higher tax band. For example, if you are in the 40 per cent tax band for the 1996/97 tax year, you may use up unused relief brought forward. You may also pay a premium in the following year and relate it back to 1996/97 if, for any reason, you were not able to pay it in the actual year. (See Example 5, page 145.)

Other payments

Make sure that if you make payments which are allowable as relief, you do claim them. You may, for instance, have been paying maintenance but not claiming it. If there are any such payments, you may be able to claim for up to six years' back claims.

TAKING ADVANTAGE OF EXEMPTIONS

Several types of income are exempt from tax. There are nearly 30 items of exempt income including special exemptions for people like miners and Members of Parliament.

Most of these exemptions are things over which you have no control, so that there is not much scope for using them to minimise

You are a married man, self employed and your business makes an abnormally large profit of £50,000, which is taxable in 1996/97. You are already paying £500 per year in pension premiums. Your tax position for the year is as follows:

	£	£
Profits		50,000
Pension premiums	500	
Personal relief	3,765	
		4,265
Taxable		45,735
Tax due		
20% x 3,900		780.00
24% x 21,600		5,184.00
40% x 20,235		8,094.00
		14,058.00
Married couple's allowance 1790 x 15%		268.50
		13,789.50
Class 4 National Insurance	50,000	
Lower limit	6,860	
	43,140	
Maximum 6% x	16,800	1008.00
Total liability		14,797.50

If you are aged 40, and paying personal pension scheme premiums, the maximum limit for the year would be 20% of £50,000 – *ie* £10,000. As you have already paid £500, you may pay another £9,500 in the 1996/97 tax year, or in the 1997/98 tax year, and elect to relate it back to the 1996/97 tax year. If you took full advantage of that, you would get tax relief at 40% on those extra premiums, but still be paying tax at 40% on £10,735. If you can afford the extra premium, and you had sufficient unused relief brought forward, you could pay that much extra premium and get tax relief at 40%. You could, of course, pay more, if you had sufficient unused relief brought forward, but you would then only get the tax relief at the lower 24% and 20% tax rate.

Example 5.

your tax. However, there are some exempt items which you do have control over, and which the government has encouraged you to use.

Personal equity plans

These were set up by the government some years ago to encourage investment. You may invest in a general PEP up to £6,000 in each tax year, and a further £3,000 in a single company PEP in each tax year.

Most of the PEPs on offer at present are from unit trusts or investment trusts, under the general PEP allowance. The single company PEPs are, as their name suggests, investments in one company under a PEP which that company has set up.

All income under PEPs are free from income tax, and any gains on selling them are free from capital gains tax. They should be looked upon as a longer term investment, since the charges of the plan managers in the first couple of years usually swallow up any tax advantage.

TESSAs

These are tax exempt special savings accounts, again set up by the government some years ago to encourage saving. These are interest bearing accounts, and have certain restrictions. You may invest up to £3,000 in the first year, then up to £1,800 in any following year up to a total of £9,000 maximum. The account must be kept for five years to get the benefit of the tax free status. You may withdraw the interest in those five years, but you may not withdraw any of the capital without losing the tax free status.

Certain Government Stocks for non-residents

If you are non-resident in the UK for any year the interest from the following government stocks is exempt from tax.

9% Conversion 2000	7.75% Treasury 2006
9% Conversion 2011	7.75% Treasury 2012/15
9.5% Conversion 2001	8% Treasury 2003
9.75% Conversion 2003	8% Treasury 2002/6
7% Treasury Convertible 1997	8% Treasury 2013
2.5% Treasury Index-linked 2024	8.5% Treasury 2000
4.125% Treasury Index-linked 2030	8.5% Treasury 2007
4.375% Treasury Index-linked 2004	8.75% Treasury 1997
4.625% Treasury Index-linked 1998	8.75% Treasury 2017
5.5% Treasury 2008/12	9% Treasury 2008
6% Treasury 1999	9% Treasury 2012
6.25% Treasury 2010	9.5% Treasury 1999
6.75% Treasury 1995/98	13.25% Treasury 1997
6.75% Treasury 2004	15.5% Treasury 1998
7% Treasury 2001	3.5% War Loan
7.25% Treasury 1998	Floating Rate Treasury 1999

Certain National Savings Interest
- The first £70 each year of interest on National Savings Ordinary Accounts is exempt from tax.
- All interest on National Savings Certificates is exempt from tax.
- All interest on Save As You Earn schemes is exempt from tax.

TIMING YOUR TRANSACTIONS

It is occasionally possible to reduce your tax bill by the timing of your transactions. Obviously, this is only possible where you have control over your income. The reason for doing this would be to move income from one year when your tax rate is higher into another year when your tax rate is lower, or from one year when the allowances are lower to another year when the allowances are higher.

Closing a building society account
You may, for instance, want to bring some income forward to the current year. If you have a building society account, you could close the account before the end of the tax year. The building society then credits you with interest on the date you close the account, instead of at the next yearly or half yearly date. You have then brought some interest back into the current year.

Of course, you must make sure that you do not incur any penalty by closing your building society account. You must also be sure that you can reinvest the money in a new building society account or other form of investment giving at least as good an interest rate as the one you closed.

Limiting capital allowance claims
Another example occurs if you are in business. It may be possible to limit your claim for capital allowances and thus pay more this year when your tax rate is lower, but then be able to claim more capital allowances next year when your tax rate is higher.

Selling investments
If you have investments, and you actively manage them, it is also possible to control the timing of your sales of investments, which may have a bearing on your capital gains tax. You have an allowance of £6,300 for 1996/97 before any capital gains tax becomes payable.

Bed and breakfast

Thus, if you are approaching the end of a tax year, and you have not yet used up your allowance, you may be able to sell an investment to produce a gain that still keeps you within your threshold allowance. Of course, sales of investments must be made on good grounds, not just for the purpose of saving some tax. If there is no investment that you have a good reason to sell, you could carry out a 'Bed and Breakfast' transaction. This involves selling an investment and buying it back the next day. You have then realised the gain (if any) up to the date you sold it, and your purpose has been achieved. You must balance against this, however, the costs of carrying out the 'Bed and Breakfast' transaction (the stockbrokers' commission).

Establishing a loss

You may also want to do a 'Bed and Breakfast' transaction to establish a loss rather than a profit. This might be advantageous when you are approaching the end of a tax year, and you have already carried out transactions producing a gain more than the threshold allowance. You can then carry out a 'Bed and Breakfast' to reduce the gain to an amount lower than your allowance.

This same tactic may also be used to reduce the rate of tax. Capital gains tax is charged by adding it to your other income and calculating the extra tax that would be payable. It is therefore effectively taxed as the top slice of your income, and could take you into higher rates. Therefore, if you are approaching the end of a tax year, and you know that you have already made capital gains which will be taxed at a higher rate, you may carry out a 'Bed and Breakfast' to reduce your gain to an amount which will keep it in the lower rate of tax.

QUESTIONS AND ANSWERS

If I can save tax by paying my wife a salary from my business, why not save even more by paying my children?

Wages paid from your business must reflect the commercial reality. If you have, say, teenage children working for your business, you may pay them. But their wages should not be artificially inflated. They should reflect what you would normally pay others of the same age, doing the same job, for the same number of hours.

CASE STUDIES

Anthony creates a partnership

Anthony is employing his wife at a modest salary of £1,000 per year. He takes advice from his accountant, and because of the involvement of his wife in the business he makes her into a partner. Their tax position before and after the change is as follows:

		Before			*After*	
		Husband	*Wife*		*Husband*	*Wife*
		£	£		£	£
Business profit		13,000			7,000	7,000
Salary			1,000			
Building society interest		400	100		400	100
Dividends		200			200	
		13,600	1,100		7,600	7,100
Personal allowance	3,765		3,765	3,765		3,765
Pension premium	500			500		
		4,265			4,265	
Taxable		9,335	NIL		3,335	3,335
Tax due						
20% x 3,900		780.00	20% x 3,335		667.00	667.00
20% x 600		120.00				
24% x 4,835		1,160.40				
		2,060.40				
Married couple's allowance		268.50			268.50	
		1,791.90			398.50	

Class 4 National Insurance

Profit	13,000		Profit	7,000		
Limit	6,860		Limit	6,860		
6% x 6,140	368.40		6% x140		8.40	8.40
	2,160.30				406.90	675.40
		Total tax				1,082.30

There has been a tax saving of £1,078.

Max equalises income and uses exemptions

Max and his wife have the following incomes for 1996/97:

Husband	£
Company pension	10,000
State pension	4,000
Bank interest	100
Building society interest	200
Share dividends	2,500
Unit trust dividends	1,000
Total income	17,800

Wife	£
State pension	3,200
Building society interest	100
National Savings Bonds	350
Unit trust dividends	250
Total income	3,900

Max transfers all the shares to his wife, cashes in £12,000 of the unit trusts, buys a Personal Equity Plan of £6,000 for himself, and one for his wife, and transfers the other £8,000 of unit trusts to his wife. He keeps the bank account in his name, but transfers all the building society accounts to his wife's name. The income stays the same, but the saving in tax is shown below.

	Before			*After*	
	Husband	*Wife*		*Husband*	*Wife*
	£	£		£	£
Company pension	10,000			10,000	
State pension	4,000	3,200		4,000	3,200
Bank interest	100			100	
Building society interest	200	100			300
National Savings		350			350
Share dividends	2,500				2,500
Unit trust dividends	1,000	250			650
Total	17,800	3,900		14,100	7,000
Age allowance restricted	3,790				
Age allowance		4,910		5,090	4,910
Taxable	14,010	NIL		9,010	2,090

Tax due					
20% x 3,900	780.00		20% x 3,900	780.00	
20% x 3,800	760.00		20% x 100	20.00	
24% x 6,310	1,514.40		20% x 2,090		418.00
			24% x 5,010	1,202.40	
	3,054.40			2,002.40	418.00
Married couple's allowance	473.25			473.25	
				1,529.15	418.00
Total tax	2,581.15				1,947.15

There has been a tax saving of £634.

DISCUSSION POINTS

1. Can you and your spouse equalise your income? Are there any other factors which might affect the way you share your money?

2. What items of your income do you have control over? Can you use them to save tax?

3. How does your attitude to investment risk affect your savings? Are there any tax exempt forms of savings or investments which you could take advantage of?

11
Important Dates and Deadlines

DEADLINES

Sending in your tax return

If you want the Inspector of Taxes to calculate your tax
The later of:

- 30 September following the end of the tax year, and
- two months after the tax return is issued.

If you want to calculate your tax
The later of:

- 31 January following the end of the tax year, and
- three months after the tax return is issued.

Revision of your tax return

By you
Twelve months from normal filing date.

By the Inspector of Taxes
Nine months from receipt of the tax return.

Notification of enquiry
Twelve months from normal filing date.

Retaining your records

If you are in business or have income from property
Five years from the latest date for filing the tax return.

If you are undergoing an enquiry
When the Inspector of Taxes tells you that you may discard your records.

Any other cases
One year from the latest date for filing the tax return.

DATES

5 April 1997	End of the 1996/97 tax year.
6 April 1997	Tax returns sent out by Inland Revenue.
31 May 1997	Your employer must provide you with a P60 for the year ended 5 April 1997.
6 July 1997	Your employer must provide you with details of the P11D for the year ended 5 April 1997.
31 July 1997	Pay second payment on account for 1996/97.
30 September 1997	Send your 1997 tax return in if you want the Inspector of Taxes to calculate your tax.
5 October 1997	Notify Inland Revenue if you have income to declare for the year ended 5 April 1997 but you have not received a tax return.
31 January 1998	Pay first payment on account for 1997/98. Pay balancing payment for 1996/97. Final date for sending in your 1997 tax return if it was issued to you before 1 November 1997.
5 April 1998	End of 1997/98 tax year.
6 April 1998	Tax returns sent out by Inland Revenue.
31 May 1998	Your employer must provide you with a P60 for the year ended 5 April 1998.
6 July 1998	Your employer must provide you with details of the P11D for the year ended 5 April 1998.
31 July 1998	Pay second payment on account for 1997/98.
30 September 1998	Send your 1998 tax return in if you want the Inspector of Taxes to calculate your tax.
5 October 1998	Notify Inland Revenue if you have income to declare for the year ended 5 April 1998 but you have not received a tax return.
31 January 1999	You may now dispose of records for the year ended 5 April 1997 if you sent your tax return in on time, and if there is no enquiry going on unless you are self employed or have property income. Pay first payment on account of 1998/99 tax. Pay balancing amount of 1997/98 tax. Final date for sending in your 1998 tax return if it was issued before 1 November 1998.

Glossary

Capital allowances. These are allowances given against tax for assets used in your self employment or in your employment. The allowance given is one quarter of the costs in the first year. That allowance is deducted, then one quarter of the remaining balance deducted in the next year and so on.

Capital gains tax. A tax on profits made on selling assets or on 'sums derived from assets'. The assessment is made on the profit less an allowance for inflation, and after deducting a personal threshold.

Charitable covenants. A covenant is a legally binding promise to pay a certain amount. By entering into a covenant with a registered charity for a period of four years, the charity may reclaim tax on the amount you pay.

Coding notice. A statement sent to all people taxed under PAYE showing your allowances and any adjustments (such as untaxed interest which partly uses up the personal allowance). This then gives a figure of allowances to set against your income. This is translated into a code number (which is the number of the allowances divided by ten). This code number is used by your employer to work out your tax for your pay period (usually weekly or monthly).

Commissioners. The General Commissioners are an independent tribunal of locally appointed people who arbitrate between taxpayers and the Inland Revenue. There are many of these - at least one per tax district. They meet at regular intervals to decide on matters brought before them. You have the right to appeal to them. Their decision is considered as final on matters of fact. Another body of specially appointed lawyers is called the Special Commissioners. They are also independent, but are only called upon to decide matters of law, as opposed to matters of fact.

CSA. Child Support Agency: the government body which directs how much divorced or separated fathers should pay for their children's support.

PAYE. Pay as you earn: the system by which employed people have their tax deducted at source. Your employer is supplied with a set of tables by the Inland Revenue by which (in conjunction with your code number) your tax is calculated and deducted from your wages.

PEP. Personal Equity Plan: a special tax-exempt investment incentive set up by the government. All income and capital gains are tax free.

P11D. This is a statement from your employer to the Inspector of Taxes showing the amount of any benefits in kind you have received for the tax year, and any expenses reimbursed to you. Some of these expenses may be claimable by you. Your employer must give you a copy of these amounts by 6 July following the end of the tax year.

P45. This is a document given to you when you leave a job in the middle of a tax year. It shows your pay from the beginning of the tax year to the date you left, tax deducted up to that date, and your code number. You should hand it to your new employer or to the Department of Social Security Benefits Agency if you claim unemployment benefit.

P60. This is a statement given to you by your employer at the end of the tax year, showing your total pay for the tax year, tax deducted, and your final code number. It also shows the tax reference of your employer, and the amount of National Insurance contributions you have paid for the year. Your employer must give you this by 31 May following the end of the tax year.

P160. This is a statement given to you by your employer when you retire from employment but go straight on to their pension scheme.

R185. A certificate issued by trustees or executors. It certifies the income and the tax deducted.

TESSA. Tax Exempt Special Savings Account. A special savings account introduced by the government. With certain restrictions, the account is tax free. Most banks and building societies have their own versions.

Index

How To Books provide practical help on a large range of topics. They are available through all good bookshops or can be ordered direct from the distributors. Just tick the titles you want and complete the form on the following page.

___ Apply to an Industrial Tribunal (£7.99)	___ Getting That Job (£8.99)
___ Applying for a Job (£8.99)	___ Getting your First Job (£8.99)
___ Applying for a United States Visa (£15.99)	___ Going to University (£8.99)
___ Backpacking Round Europe (£8.99)	___ Helping your Child to Read (£8.99)
___ Be a Freelance Journalist (£8.99)	___ How to Study & Learn (£8.99)
___ Be a Freelance Secretary (£8.99)	___ Investing in People (£9.99)
___ Become a Freelance Sales Agent (£9.99)	___ Investing in Stocks & Shares (£9.99)
___ Become an Au Pair (£8.99)	___ Keep Business Accounts (£7.99)
___ Becoming a Father (£8.99)	___ Know Your Rights at Work (£8.99)
___ Buy & Run a Shop (£8.99)	___ Live & Work in America (£9.99)
___ Buy & Run a Small Hotel (£8.99)	___ Live & Work in Australia (£12.99)
___ Buying a Personal Computer (£9.99)	___ Live & Work in Germany (£9.99)
___ Career Networking (£8.99)	___ Live & Work in Greece (£9.99)
___ Career Planning for Women (£8.99)	___ Live & Work in Italy (£8.99)
___ Cash from your Computer (£9.99)	___ Live & Work in New Zealand (£9.99)
___ Choosing a Nursing Home (£9.99)	___ Live & Work in Portugal (£9.99)
___ Choosing a Package Holiday (£8.99)	___ Live & Work in the Gulf (£9.99)
___ Claim State Benefits (£9.99)	___ Living & Working in Britain (£8.99)
___ Collecting a Debt (£9.99)	___ Living & Working in China (£9.99)
___ Communicate at Work (£7.99)	___ Living & Working in Hong Kong (£10.99)
___ Conduct Staff Appraisals (£7.99)	___ Living & Working in Israel (£10.99)
___ Conducting Effective Interviews (£8.99)	___ Living & Working in Saudi Arabia (£12.99)
___ Coping with Self Assessment (£9.99)	___ Living & Working in the Netherlands (£9.99)
___ Copyright & Law for Writers (£8.99)	___ Making a Complaint (£8.99)
___ Counsel People at Work (£7.99)	___ Making a Wedding Speech (£8.99)
___ Creating a Twist in the Tale (£8.99)	___ Manage a Sales Team (£8.99)
___ Creative Writing (£9.99)	___ Manage an Office (£8.99)
___ Critical Thinking for Students (£8.99)	___ Manage Computers at Work (£8.99)
___ Dealing with a Death in the Family (£9.99)	___ Manage People at Work (£8.99)
___ Do Voluntary Work Abroad (£8.99)	___ Manage Your Career (£8.99)
___ Do Your Own Advertising (£8.99)	___ Managing Budgets & Cash Flows (£9.99)
___ Do Your Own PR (£8.99)	___ Managing Meetings (£8.99)
___ Doing Business Abroad (£10.99)	___ Managing Your Personal Finances (£8.99)
___ Doing Business on the Internet (£12.99)	___ Managing Yourself (£8.99)
___ Emigrate (£9.99)	___ Market Yourself (£8.99)
___ Employ & Manage Staff (£8.99)	___ Master Book-Keeping (£8.99)
___ Find Temporary Work Abroad (£8.99)	___ Mastering Business English (£8.99)
___ Finding a Job in Canada (£9.99)	___ Master GCSE Accounts (£8.99)
___ Finding a Job in Computers (£8.99)	___ Master Public Speaking (£8.99)
___ Finding a Job in New Zealand (£9.99)	___ Migrating to Canada (£12.99)
___ Finding a Job with a Future (£8.99)	___ Obtaining Visas & Work Permits (£9.99)
___ Finding Work Overseas (£9.99)	___ Organising Effective Training (£9.99)
___ Freelance DJ-ing (£8.99)	___ Pass Exams Without Anxiety (£7.99)
___ Freelance Teaching & Tutoring (£9.99)	___ Passing That Interview (£8.99)
___ Get a Job Abroad (£10.99)	___ Plan a Wedding (£7.99)
___ Get a Job in America (£9.99)	___ Planning Your Gap Year (£8.99)
___ Get a Job in Australia (£9.99)	___ Prepare a Business Plan (£8.99)
___ Get a Job in Europe (£9.99)	___ Publish a Book (£9.99)
___ Get a Job in France (£9.99)	___ Publish a Newsletter (£9.99)
___ Get a Job in Travel & Tourism (£8.99)	___ Raise Funds & Sponsorship (£7.99)
___ Get into Radio (£8.99)	___ Rent & Buy Property in France (£9.99)
___ Getting into Films & Television (£10.99)	___ Rent & Buy Property in Italy (£9.99)

___ Research Methods (£8.99)	___ Use the Internet (£9.99)
___ Retire Abroad (£8.99)	___ Winning Consumer Competitions (£8.99)
___ Return to Work (£7.99)	___ Winning Presentations (£8.99)
___ Run a Voluntary Group (£8.99)	___ Work from Home (£8.99)
___ Setting up Home in Florida (£9.99)	___ Work in an Office (£7.99)
___ Spending a Year Abroad (£8.99)	___ Work in Retail (£8.99)
___ Start a Business from Home (£7.99)	___ Work with Dogs (£8.99)
___ Start a New Career (£6.99)	___ Working Abroad (£14.99)
___ Starting to Manage (£8.99)	___ Working as a Holiday Rep (£9.99)
___ Starting to Write (£8.99)	___ Working in Japan (£10.99)
___ Start Word Processing (£8.99)	___ Working in Photography (£8.99)
___ Start Your Own Business (£8.99)	___ Working in the Gulf (£10.99)
___ Study Abroad (£8.99)	___ Working in Hotels & Catering (£9.99)
___ Study & Live in Britain (£7.99)	___ Working on Contract Worldwide (£9.99)
___ Studying at University (£8.99)	___ Working on Cruise Ships (£9.99)
___ Studying for a Degree (£8.99)	___ Write a Press Release (£9.99)
___ Successful Grandparenting (£8.99)	___ Write a Report (£8.99)
___ Successful Mail Order Marketing (£9.99)	___ Write an Assignment (£8.99)
___ Successful Single Parenting (£8.99)	___ Write & Sell Computer Software (£9.99)
___ Survive Divorce (£8.99)	___ Write for Publication (£8.99)
___ Surviving Redundancy (£8.99)	___ Write for Television (£8.99)
___ Taking in Students (£8.99)	___ Writing a CV that Works (£8.99)
___ Taking on Staff (£8.99)	___ Writing a Non Fiction Book (£9.99)
___ Taking Your A-Levels (£8.99)	___ Writing an Essay (£8.99)
___ Teach Abroad (£8.99)	___ Writing & Publishing Poetry (£9.99)
___ Teach Adults (£8.99)	___ Writing & Selling a Novel (£8.99)
___ Teaching Someone to Drive (£8.99)	___ Writing Business Letters (£8.99)
___ Travel Round the World (£8.99)	___ Writing Reviews (£9.99)
___ Understand Finance at Work (£8.99)	___ Writing Your Dissertation (£8.99)
___ Use a Library (£7.99)	

To: Plymbridge Distributors Ltd, Plymbridge House, Estover Road, Plymouth PL6 7PZ. Customer Services Tel: (01752) 202301. Fax: (01752) 202331.

Please send me copies of the titles I have indicated. Please add postage & packing (UK £1, Europe including Eire, £2, World £3 airmail).

☐ I enclose cheque/PO payable to Plymbridge Distributors Ltd for £ [   ]

☐ Please charge to my ☐ MasterCard, ☐ Visa, ☐ AMEX card.

Account No. [   ]

Card Expiry Date [   ] 19 ☎ **Credit Card orders may be faxed or phoned.**

Customer Name (CAPITALS) ....

Address ....

.... Postcode ....

Telephone.......................... Signature ....

Every effort will be made to despatch your copy as soon as possible but to avoid possible disappointment please allow up to 21 days for despatch time (42 days if overseas). Prices and availability are subject to change without notice.

Code BPA